WITH GRACIELA TO THE
HEAD-HUNTERS

With Graciela
to the Head-hunters

ALFRED BOELDEKE

with Louis Hagen

DAVID McKAY COMPANY, INC.
NEW YORK

MADE AND PRINTED IN GREAT BRITAIN BY
ROBERT CUNNINGHAM AND SONS LTD, ALVA

CONTENTS

LIST OF ILLUSTRATIONS

facing page

NOTE: All photographs are by Alfred Boeldeke, with the following exceptions: 'Jivaro Warrior' facing page 54, ' "Tzanza" dance' and 'Jivaro building a man-trap' facing page 55

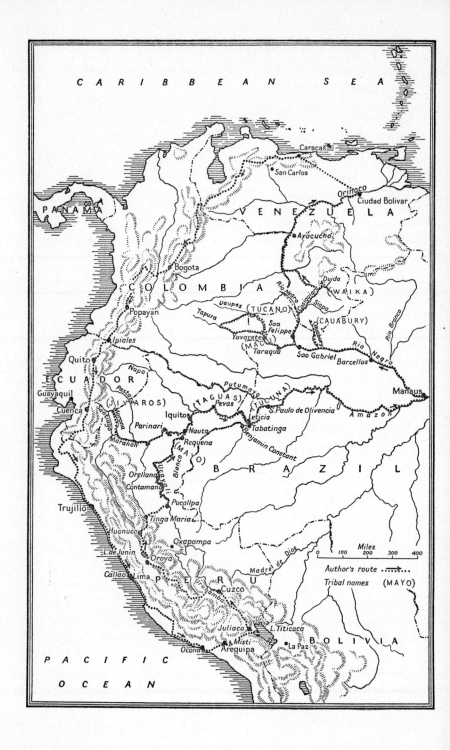

1

After Eleven Years

THE three of us stood silently in the bows of the ship as she approached the twinkling lights of La Guaira, the harbour of Caracas, Venezuela. For each of us this was perhaps the most wonderful moment of our lives and we were overflowing with emotion.

To our five-year-old daughter, Graciela, born in Germany during one of the last air raids of the war, South America was paradise on earth. This was Daddy's country where there were jungles full of mischievous monkeys and talkative parrots; where juicy fruits and bright yellow bananas grew on trees; where the sun always shone and no one had to worry about clothes; where children spent their days fishing in canoes or hunting with bows and arrows; where meals were eaten around blazing fires and where everyone slept in the open. Graciela had heard about it from her 'Papi', and she had taken it for granted that one day she would live in South America where life would be wonderful.

For Aenne, the wife I married in Germany in 1942, it was like being a bride again. The beauty and richness of the simple life along the Amazon was probably the first thing I ever talked to her about. Our married life during the war had been only a period of transition for her, a time of waiting and preparation for the life we had planned together in South America. This was the only thing that had kept her going during the war, her only hope for the future, her only comfort in the cruel world that crumbled around her. And now she stood beside me like a bride whose long, precarious engagement was coming to an end and she was following her husband to a new and happy life.

For me it was a home-coming after eleven long and wasted years. I had been passionately longing to return to this hemisphere ever since 1939. I had gone to Germany to see my parents and to arrange some business affairs; then the war started and I was not allowed to return to South America. I was thirty years old and I was called up. Since I had no feelings whatsoever for the thousand-year Reich, which the war was supposed to defend, I made it my business to keep out of the armed forces. I was drafted as a captain's steward into the Merchant Marines and I spent a busy war shuttling back and forth along the Baltic coast in small rickety freighters. I was bombed and shipwrecked many times. I lost six ships in all and was awarded a rather minor medal for managing to keep alive.

After the war Aenne and I moved to Munich where we started a newspaper clipping service, supplying newspaper cuttings to industry, political parties, ministries and the offices of foreign military governments. Although our business grew rapidly we were obsessed by the idea of saving enough money to be amongst the first batch of emigrants to leave for South America.

I had first come to Brazil when I was barely fifteen years old. I was a ship's cabin boy and we landed, after a rough crossing from Hamburg, in Buenos Aires. Our freight had included the famous Hagenbeck Circus and we carried huge crates and boxes full of live animals, from lions to little monkeys.

I remember the first mate saying to me:

'Can't you keep away from the monkeys and get to work? They aren't that much different from you—just as bone lazy. But they can climb better and they eat a hell-of-a-lot less.'

'But they don't get a hiding either,' I said, looking at the piece of rope that he carried.

Then I scampered off to work, reflecting that life must be best where there aren't any first mates, only Indians with blow-pipes, monkeys swinging from branch to branch, and where one is one's own master to do as one pleases.

So in Buenos Aires I decided to let the good ship *Artus* blow its lungs out calling 'All Aboard', and stayed behind to seek adventure. When the *Artus* was starting on her long voyage

home, I was squatting in an empty cattle truck, dressed in the
Boy Scout's uniform which I had smuggled ashore, rolling
through the endless Argentine Pampas towards the west.

Almost starved, without knowing a single word of Spanish, I
arrived at Mendoza at the foot of the vast Andes. I stayed there
for a few months working as a kitchen boy in a roadside café,
learning Spanish and recovering from the privations of the
journey.

Soon the urge for the unknown drove me off again and I
crossed the eighteen thousand-feet-high pass over the Andes into
Chile. It was stormy and snowing hard and my worn shoes fell
to pieces. I tore my shirt into shreds and wrapped my naked feet
in the rags. This way I reached the other side of the mountains,
half frozen, but still alive.

I stayed for some months in Northern Chile and worked in an
ore mine where a friendly Swiss engineer arranged an apprentice-
ship for me in the machine shop of the mine. But I wanted to
see the whole of South America and was thirsty for more adventure, so I set off once more, still wearing my Boy Scout's uniform.
I carried a sign, 'On foot around the world', which encouraged
many people to give me lifts in carts or carriages. I took any
work that was going and saved stamps from every place I passed.
I dragged heavy mailbags into the interior, collected rubber in
the Bolivian jungle, washed gold, went hunting with the native
Indians, canoed down rapids and travelled through the deepest
unexplored jungles of Brazil, Paraguay, Bolivia and Peru. Without knowing it I grew up to become a vagabond of the jungle. I
got to know and understand many of the mysteries of its plants,
animals and weather; the jungle became my home and in it I
felt safe and completely self-sufficient. I also learned to study
people and their environment and how to get on with men,
whatever their race or background. The more I learned about
the jungle, the more it fascinated me. As other young men
might be passionately drawn to science, drama, engineering, I
· was in love with the jungle and the people who populated it.

During the next few years I crossed and recrossed South
America several times, on foot, horseback, by mule and in dug-

outs. I became a jungle guide to many expeditions in search of diamonds and oil, I tried to follow the trail of Colonel Fawcett to discover the mystery of his disappearance, and spent almost a year on the Galapagos Islands, off the coast of Ecuador, trying to throw light on the murder of the Berlin doctor, Ritter, and the disappearance of the Franco-Austrian Baroness Bosquet de Wagner and her lover. Then came the sad years of forced residence in Germany.

Now with a wife and a child, I had at last returned to the life and country I had never stopped calling home.

We stayed for six months in Caracas, but we never looked on it as anything but a 'half-way house' on our road to adventure. The outfit for our journey and the fares had taken everything I had saved. But I had something which most people have lost nowadays—time and patience. I needed neither during the first few months for the streets of Caracas seemed paved with gold. To start with I toured the swankiest night-clubs with a camera which developed and printed pictures instantaneously. I worked every night non-stop and made a lot of money, which I hoped would help me to escape from the stuffy night-clubs into the steaming wilderness of the jungle.

With the first thousand bolivars I earned I equipped a modest souvenir and lampshade factory. I used hardwoods from the jungle and turned them into objects which I copied from the primitive tribes of the jungle. Before long I had more orders than I could handle. I was on my way to becoming a successful businessman, but I put a stop to this drift towards respectability and sold out when business was at its best.

From then onwards my friends in Caracas called me the *loco* —the madman. They felt further confirmed in their judgment when I bought an eight-year-old-van, removed the body, and replaced it with a jungle hut of plaited palm leaves. With this contraption, which was much sturdier than it looked, we set out on our long journey. It was spring 1951.

'You must be mad,' people called after us, but we did not hear them. At last I was on my way again, but this time with a family and a portable home. Whoever has the urge and the courage to make a long and uncomfortable journey, may have the vehicle as a present; it is parked near the sources of the Amazon, where the last signs of the road merge with the jungle.

We drove inland from Caracas towards the Colombian border, singing, whistling and very happy. Our exultant mood did not last for long, for towards evening we had our first breakdown. The car was overloaded and a spring went. When that had been replaced the next day and we had been driving for an hour a tyre burst. I cursed and struggled on the hot dusty road to change the tyre and began to wonder how we could possibly cope with the thousands of miles of rough roads, jungle and desert tracks and mountain passes before us. Aenne must have had the same doubts because she asked me to stop at a small chapel just before the pass began to climb steeply up the side of a ravine strewn with crosses. We bought and lit a candle in honour of the saint who protects travellers and watched it burn brightly among the many others left by passing motorists.

Usually we did not care where we stopped for the night so long as there was water nearby. Aenne had to cook inside the little hut since the wind along the Andes, which we followed almost the entire time, was very strong. It was also more comfortable to eat inside. A table was folded down, a cloth spread out and it was Graciela's joy to surprise us with a bunch of flowers which she proudly arranged in the vase in the middle of the table. We had ample room in our jungle hut on wheels which had two bunks fixed one on top of the other. Graciela's bed, on which she slept perfectly, was made from a car seat.

As we travelled further into the interior and reached the Colombian mountain villages, white people seemed rare visitors. A crowd of children, and even adults, was always on our trail when we went shopping. The children used to talk excitedly amongst themselves and especially admired our fair little daughter. As soon as I bought a bottle of cognac in one of the village shops the ice was broken and the men and women became talkative and wanted to know all about us.

The road through the Colombian Andes was a good one and

was bordered by endless pastures on which vast cattle herds grazed. It continued like this as far as Bogota, the capital of Colombia, where we stayed a fortnight. We found it a friendly and agreeable city although it rained the whole time we were there. We were amazed at the cheapness of everything compared with Venezuela.

Leaving Bogota we passed through the lovely Valle de Cauca to Popayan, the beautiful old university town of Colombia, and crossed into Ecuador at Ipiales. Not far inside the border we met our first Quechua Indians. The men of this tribe wear their hair in long pigtails, but scuttled away like rabbits when we tried to photograph them.

Driving on a fairly good cobblestone road through the rocky landscape that makes up part of the highlands of Ecuador, we were suddenly faced with a huge globe of the Earth hewn from rock. This marks the spot of *el medio mundo*—the middle of the earth or the Equator. It was very lonely, except for an old Indian woman who sat wrapped in her *poncho* on the pedestal of the globe. A cold wind blew down the bare rock and we, too, put on our jackets. When we turned to continue our journey south and the old woman murmured *'que les vaya muy bien'* and crossed herself, we felt elated and rather festive.

Now we were in the southern hemisphere and soon came to Quito, the capital of Ecuador. Although Quito was not a very exciting place, we spent a few weeks there to give Graciela a rest and my wife a chance to give her some lessons. It also allowed me to replenish our empty cash box by selling lampshades and souvenirs. Graciela had been to school for several months in Caracas and the teacher, who thought she was a bright little girl, was disappointed when we took her away. We did not feel too worried about it since Aenne was going to teach her during our long journey. But until now there had been so much to see and so many fresh impressions to absorb that it had seemed wrong to burden her little brain still further with numbers and the alphabet. Besides when we stopped for the night Aenne had had the cooking, laundry and other household chores to do and the moment I got out of the car to walk to the nearest village to

The author with Graciela (left)

*'House on wheels' and Graciela
in front of Arequipa Cathedral*

Old Spanish doorway, Cuzco

Mountain road, Ecuador (see page 6)

Llamas near Lake Titicaca

shop or scrounge, Graciela was at my side. It would have broken her heart had I not let her come on these expeditions.

We enjoyed our three weeks of immobility at Quito. Graciela loved her lessons and made friends with the children of the neighbourhood. She tried to teach them to ride her little bicycle which she insisted on taking with us everywhere. She showed off with all sorts of tricks such as racing down a steep hill without holding the handlebars, a performance which impressed her friends but greatly worried us. A plague of fleas almost drove us to desperation and we could not get rid of them whatever we did. When we spoke to the locals about it they laughed and assured us that there was nothing like it in Quito. They were so used to the insects that they did not realise that the entire place was jumping.

This prolonged stay had been an exception so far on our trip. Although we generally took it easy and did not drive more than sixty miles a day, we seldom stopped in one place for very long. We were always pressing on in quest of new experiences and feared we would miss something if we wasted too much time. At the back of our minds there was the feeling that this part of our journey, however interesting, was not what we were searching for. It was only the route leading to the interior, to the places where the jungle was thickest and nature unspoilt, where primitive life still held the mystery and richness which civilisation had never been able to replace.

A month later, after a wonderful drive through almost the entire length of Ecuador and Peru, with the blue Pacific ocean on one side and the snow-clad Andes on the other, we reached a small place called Ocoña. Here Graciela was in heaven building outsized sand-castles and ordering the local children to fetch and carry for her, and Aenne did a little mending and cooking between bathing and dozing on the beach. I spent my days going out with the fishermen, harpooning giant fish, sea-lions and seals.

2

Fortunato

THE fishermen often talked about the *loco*—the mad-one —of Ocoña; they believed he was in league with the ghosts and spirits and he both fascinated and frightened them. One morning as I was returning from my daily visit to the old Indian woman who brewed my sugar-cane schnapps, I saw a figure lying at the edge of a rice field that I knew, at first glance, must be this man. Fortunato was lying on his back, staring thoughtfully into the cloudless sky, and I felt sure he had chosen this discreet spot, which I was known to pass every day, to wait for me. No doubt he had heard of me as the mad *gringo* who would follow the fish to their grottoes under the sea, and felt instinctively that he and I had something in common.

I stretched out beside him and gave him a cigarette; for some time neither of us spoke, then I offered him a swig from my bottle and he mumbled something in his Quechuas tongue which I could not understand. He drank but showed no signs of breaking his silence, so, like him, I continued to stare up into the sky, only looking at him from time to time out of the corner of my eye. But his red-brown Indian face was impenetrable. Then I had an idea: the tree which was protecting us from the scorching sun was a willow, and willow wands make the best divining rods. I got up, cut off a branch and demonstrated the powers of the 'dowser' over the waters of the rice field.

Fortunato was impressed. 'You are the right man for me,' he said, now speaking in broken Spanish, 'Yes, you are the right man, you have contact with the spirits.' Then he told me a fantastic story.

8

'A day and a half from here by donkey,' he began, 'in the same valley as the river that flows quietly not far from where we are now lying, there is a forgotten village completely covered by earth and lava. A thousand years ago an Inca army invaded this region from the mountains and reached the outskirts of this prosperous settlement.

'The leader of the Inca army called the villagers together and told them that it was the will of the Sun God that they all must die. Some were beheaded by the Incas and the rest were told to kill themselves.

'After the army had departed, the villagers gathered together for a feast to celebrate their imminent departure from their earthly lives. They brewed masses of *chicha*—maize beer—and danced and sang and made love until they were utterly exhausted. Then everyone, young and old alike, drank a deadly poison with their last bowl of beer, wrapped themselves in pieces of cloth and waited to die.'

Fortunato paused and looked at me with cunning eyes. When he saw that I was deep in thought, letting the whole ghastly scene pass in front of my closed eyes, he again relapsed into silence and once more shut himself off from me, gazing into the sky. I allowed a few minutes to pass and then once more offered him the bottle.

'Gold, lots of gold is buried there,' he mumbled. 'I have been there many times and dug and dug, but all I have found is mummies wrapped in rags, kitchen utensils, vases, ornaments, weapons and paints. What am I to do with this rubbish? It's the treasure I am after—the treasure that I know is buried there. My father told me about it and he again was told by his father, and so on, back to the great days of the Incas. But, although we belonged to the best family, none of us could read or write.' Here Fortunato paused again, fished awkwardly in his trouser pocket and produced a curious mass of strings and ribbons.

'This handful of string holds the secret of the buried village,' he said. As he spoke he gave me a triumphant look and let the strings unfold. I watched them become a kind of net with knots at irregular intervals. 'Each knot', he whispered, 'has its meaning.' The distances between each of them was related to certain facts and memories, he explained, and the whole pattern told a chronicle of the past.

Fortunato paused again to observe the effect his story had on me. By now he could see that he had made me almost feverish with excitement so he condescended to continue.

'If you like, we will go there, but it must be within the next few days. We can approach the village only when the river is low. The rainy season is near and once the river rises we cannot get to the village for another six months.' He looked at the divining rod I was still holding in my hand. 'You are the first person apart from my family to know the secret. Perhaps your magic will make contact with the ghosts of the dead and your magic twig point to the place where the treasure is buried.'

We came to an agreement. Fortunato was to get the greater part of any treasure we found and I would have the weapons, household utensils and other things for which Fortunato had no use.

Just before sunrise the next day a small caravan quietly left Ocoña. It consisted of Fortunato, who was the leader, his brother who carried the excavation implements and his little sister, who was to be our cook and carried the pots and pans. There was also my wife, who could not keep away from any adventure, Graciela, who took it for granted that nothing could be done without her, a donkey and myself. Once we had left the huts of Ocoña behind we breathed freely again. If anyone had seen us depart we would soon have had the entire population on our heels, since Fortunato was well known as a treasure hunter and was often followed when he left the town. In spite of this he himself managed to disappear for weeks without anyone knowing where he went, though there were many rumours and fantastic tales whispered about his trips.

I now got on famously with Fortunato. We quickly became friends and this was due, I think, to my European birth. Fortunato was reserved and even suspicious with the natives and his only human contacts were with his younger brother and sister. His hut was looked after by an old wrinkled deaf woman, and occasionally he worked in his tiny rice field. During his frequent disappearances it was said that he drank from magic wells and communicated with the spirits.

Our little caravan wound itself up a valley which after a few hours narrowed and led into a deep gorge. Here we met a small group of Serranos; a mocking name meaning the high and mighty. They had come down from the fifteen thousand feet-high Andes, moving in a sharp trot all the way, carrying their agricultural produce hanging from headbands. These very primitive Indians are supposed to be the only real descendants of the Incas who centuries ago prospered on the high plateau of the mountains.

The rocky walls of the gorge now rose hundreds of feet above us and once an avalanche of stones thundered down missing us only by a few feet. The narrow oppressive walls gave us shade from the burning sun as the climb became even more strenuous, and despite our growing exhaustion and the eerie echoes from the rugged walls around us, we were happy and full of confidence, helped by the sugar-cane schnapps with which we refreshed ourselves. Just before sunset we came to a place where the gorge narrowed to a few feet. It became almost dark and we could see only a narrow slit of light high above us. At the end of the gorge a rock rising vertically for about twenty feet blocked our way, but with the help of ropes and a few steps which had been cut in the rock, we managed to climb it. Getting the donkey over this barrier was a major problem. Half of us stood on top of the rock and pulled at a rope which had been fastened round the animal's neck, while the rest stood at the bottom and tried to lift the rear end of the donkey with their shoulders. The donkey was not happy about this treatment and complained with heart-rending brays which echoed through the gorge. Eventually with a final big heave, we got him up.

We now looked down on a lovely valley gently sloping towards the snow-clad mountains. Here, under the brilliant star-studded sky, we spent the night, and by the warm glow of a fire Fortunato told us wonderful tales of his Inca ancestors.

In the chilly morning air a grey mist hung over the valley. But the coffee simmering in the kettle cheered us and we looked longingly into the purple-red dawn waiting for the first warming rays of the sun.

'It is not far now,' Fortunato said, adding that we should reach our goal before the sun reached its zenith. Encouraged and warmed we started off, my wife and I singing an old hiking-song. Graciela, as usual, had her own ideas and happily sang a different tune. So we marched along elated and as full of anticipation as if we were going to conquer the world. Even Fortunato caught our light-heartedness and we made quick progress.

The vegetation of the valley altered. The shrubs changed into trees and I excitedly showed Aenne a fig tree heavy with ripe fruit. Meanwhile she had already discovered grape vines and Graciela came running with a handful of ripe peaches. It was an unbelievable paradise and we ran hither and thither through the luscious green grass. I asked Fortunato to tell us more about this land of milk and honey, but he was restless and told me he would talk about it later when we had reached our destination. Fortunato now seemed completely changed. He grabbed the shovel from his brother with shaking hands and with feverish excitement led us on.

Soon we stood in front of an ancient ruin. The walls were coloured with the original blue and had patterns of bright yellow suns painted on them. This, Fortunato told us, was a temple in honour of the Sun God. The original Inca inhabitants had built it, but before they committed suicide they had hidden the gold and silver with which they decorated the temple. Many years later another Inca tribe settled on the same spot and rebuilt the temple, but they were all murdered during the Spanish Conquest. The Spaniards removed the gold and silver from the rebuilt temple and used most of its stones to build a Christian chapel nearby. They adorned this chapel with many of the gold ornaments they had taken and melted the silver into a huge bell for the tower.

'Masses of gold and silver have been hidden under this earth,' Fortunato told us, his eyes shining rapturously. 'The soil is good and rich fields and orchards have been harvested here for thousands of years. Yet'—and now Fortunato's voice took on a sinister

tone as he clenched his fists and lifted them towards the sun—
'this piece of earth is damned. All the people who settled here
and worked the land came to a violent death. Even the Spaniards.
After they had murdered the Incas in the most gruesome way,
more and more of them settled on this fertile land. The rich
silver mines which had been worked by the Incas were exploited
by the Spaniards. But one day a new army of Incas descended
from the Andes and there was a battle that lasted several days;
all the Spaniards were killed, leaving the monks only enough time
to hide the bell and the golden ornaments from their chapel
deep under the earth.'

By now we had left the fertile land, and were climbing over
stony ground for about a thousand feet towards a steep wall of
rocks. Half way up Fortunato dropped his shovel and threw his
poncho to the ground.

'This time I am going to start here,' he said. I looked round
but could see nothing but stones and barrenness. Fortunato
noticed my doubts and mumbled, 'You'll see soon enough.'

He began to dig, using a pick on the hard ground. After he
had gone down about three feet he stopped and ran forward
thirty yards where he started his now frantic digging again.
Then he hit something hard. It was a wooden log, about two
feet in diameter.

'An Inca house,' Fortunato shouted. He began digging again
until the bamboo roof of a house could clearly be distinguished.
Fortunato was now working as if possessed by the devil.
Suddenly the ground on which he stood gave way and he disappeared with a thud into a gaping black hole. A stinging cloud
of dust shot up and by the time it had cleared Fortunato had
climbed out and was squatting on the ground near the hole,
black from top to toe and gasping for air. I gave him a drink
from my bottle of sugar-cane schnapps.

'If you want to go down there with me', Fortunato said when
he had regained his breath, 'you had better take this.' He gave
me a handful of coca-leaves, which I chewed as one chews
tobacco. They had a bitter, unpleasant taste, which suggested
musty hay. I had a drink of schnapps and the taste improved,

but my tongue and gums went numb. Soon I felt beautifully careless, floating and happy. Nothing really mattered any longer, nothing could excite me, and I would not have worried had I been told that this was my last hour. It occurred to me that the mass suicide of the Incas buried just below us might have taken place in the same kind of cocaine delirium that I was experiencing. Perhaps their death was not so horrible after all, but a suitable ending to a mad orgy.

Using my electric torch, Fortunato climbed into the hole again and gave me a sign to follow him. In spite of the collapsed roof, the dimly-lit hollow into which I clambered was recognisable as a room. Largish bundles of various sizes were tidily arranged over the floor. Next to each bundle stood pots, pitchers and bowls filled with corn cobs and beans. There were also some wooden needles stuck into a round object bedded in wool, but I never discovered their purpose. It was apparent that the dead had been equipped with everything they might need in the beyond. The high potassium-nitrate content of the earth had conserved everything perfectly and it was as if the tragedy had happened only a short time ago.

A flash from the torch brought me out of the trance through which I had surveyed this amazing scene. Fortunato told me to carry some of the bundles and other things out through the collapsed roof. The moment I reached the air I was overcome by the most frightful pains in my head and I fainted. When I awoke my wife and all the others looked very worried, only Fortunato seemed to be at ease. There was a slightly superior smile on his face when he handed me the bottle and a few coca-leaves.

'It'll be better in a minute,' he said, and so it was. Then he explained that our discovery was only the house of poor people and hardly worth bothering about and started digging at a different point.

Meanwhile I had unwrapped the bundles. Mummy faces stared at me with hollow black eyes. I set them in a circle and took photographs. The dead Incas were obviously dressed in their best clothes and their *ponchos* were woven in striking, brightly-

coloured ornaments. The colours looked as fresh as if they had
only just left the dye-bath and the cloth was so strong that I
could not tear it. Some of the materials were cotton, some sheep-
wool and others alpaca- and llama-wool. Many of the bowls and
pots were as delicate as the finest Chinese porcelain, decorated
with ornaments and drawings of the gods in wonderfully bright
colours which had as much imagination, sense of form and colour
as a design by Picasso.

I was busy sorting out interesting examples of household
utensils when a remarkable set of teeth on one of the mummies
diverted my attention. There was something at the back of my
befuddled mind which kept my eyes glued to those teeth. Next
to me Fortunato was rummaging wildly in the dry earth and
the outline of his figure, only just visible in the dust, looked
unreal and ghostlike. The flashing teeth of the mummy still
grinned their challenge to my wits. Then I remembered a
dentist in Caracas had said he would give anything for a well-
preserved set of ancient Inca teeth.

'It shall be yours,' I said to myself, as I broke the set of teeth
carefully from the head.

I wrapped up the mummies with great care and dragged them
back to their former resting place. My heart became heavy as I
rested in complete exhaustion. You are getting old, very old, I
thought and fear came over me. Who knows how much longer
you have to live before you too will be buried in dust and darkness like those mummies. I took a piece of a *poncho* and covered
the grinning teeth beside me. I simply could not bear the sight
of them any longer.

Fortunato suddenly let loose a desperate scream and began
swearing and jumping like a mad dog. He turned towards me;
a huge thorn of a wild bamboo scrub had pierced his hand.
With a quick jerk I pulled out the thorn. A good draught of
schnapps and a few coca-leaves and we grinned at each other
again without a care in the world.

After a short rest Fortunato started work with renewed determination, '*lo encontraremos, lo encontraremos*—we will find
it, we will find it'—he screamed and the frenzy with which he

uttered these words still makes me shudder when I think of them. He tore his shirt from his chest and now stood before me almost naked, covered with sweat and dirt.

Most of the dust had now settled so that I could watch more closely his desperate movements; he had dug a small trench, about two feet deep and ten feet long. A multitude of little spikes like those which had pierced Fortunato's hand appeared at the bottom of the trench.

'Look below,' Fortunato announced, 'here is the house of a rich Inca, but it won't be easy to get at it—it's been secured by many obstacles and special walls have been built to protect it.' He was completely engrossed in his task but although he worked like a man possessed, he was careful. After the spikes had been laid bare he reached a layer of carefully arranged stones which had sharp edges pointing upwards. Dirt was running down his neck, but the sugar-cane schnapps gave him new impetus when he tired and the cocaine leaves gave him endurance. He just could not give up now that he was so close to success.

Then he was stopped in his progress by a thick wooden beam; he moved it and we saw to our amazement that a piece of matting was fixed to it, and this hung vertically down into the earth; it was obviously the door to a room. Now it became easier for Fortunato to dig deeper for the stone walls had been pierced and loose dust took their place. Again his spade struck resistance, so he dropped his shovel and started groping with his hand. He pulled, and slowly a severed head intact with skin and hair, appeared. Fortunato continued digging, unearthing head after head. I arranged these heads in a hollow as fast as he handed them to me.

At last the schnapps and the coca-leaves lost their potency for Fortunato and he climbed wearily out of the hole. His mongol face was bloated and had become a bluish-yellow; his head looked gruesomely like those of the dead Incas lying around us. A man with death written all over his face!

But he would not rest long. 'I must go down again,' he insisted, after another dose of schnapps and coca-leaves. He returned to the hole and freed the vertical matting. As he pulled it away with a sharp tug an Inca mummy toppled over and fell against him with a thud. Both collapsed on the floor and a horrified scream rising out of the cloud of dust brought Fortunato's brother and sister, my wife and Graciela running to the spot. But the only fatal casualty was the Inca: Fortunato seemed only a little shocked. The sugar-cane schnapps made its rounds again, God knows how many times, until we had all recovered.

I managed to drag the Inca out of the hole, bent double but in one piece, and took a photograph. His hair was fair and his face was still covered with flesh and skin. He seemed so alive with his hands holding a catapult ready to fire that Fortunato had almost died from the shock of meeting this blond giant who had been posted so many hundreds of years ago to guard the sacred home.

By now, even Fortunato had had enough and we decided to settle down for the night, but, to me at least, it brought little rest. Mobs of wildly screaming Incas, their stone catapults at the ready, surged down on us in my dreams and I saw myself trampled to death by their naked feet, and through the dreams came the desperate screams of Fortunato. He had a very high fever and the wound in his hand had become septic; the spike might well have been poisoned and a slow agonising death could be the result; anything could be expected from the magic of these ancient people. Whatever it was, poor Fortunato paid during this one night for the sins of his entire life. His feverish delirium and cries for help were so distressing that none of us wished to continue the search for the treasure and only longed for daybreak so that we could escape from this cursed part of the earth.

As soon as dawn broke we tied the now unconscious Fortunato to the back of the donkey and, like the remnants of a beaten army, made our way home. We travelled again through the fertile paradise, but this time it was as if all the fruits were poisoned and, driven by an undefinable fear, we hurried on. When Fortunato regained consciousness he demanded energetically to be taken off the donkey. The sight of a huge old olive tree standing in a strategic position between the Sun-temple of the

Incas and the chapel built by the Spanish monks gave him renewed energy. We lifted him to the ground and he swayed and stumbled into the chapel where he unearthed the remains of the altar and pieces of a large crucifix. He was convinced that the altar jewels and ornaments were hidden close by.

He shook with fever as he mumbled, 'An ancient olive tree . . . underneath the olive tree . . . I saw it all in my dreams last night, just as it was hundreds of years ago. The Spaniards were defending themselves desperately against a brave Inca army which destroyed them to the last man. Just before the end a monk and two sturdy Spanish soldiers hid the heavy silver bell, together with the bejewelled altar pieces, under the olive tree. You will see I am right, I saw every detail of it last night in my dreams.'

Fortunato stared in front of him so wildly that I feared for the remnants of his sanity. Had the shock and the high fever driven him completely mad?

'Give me the spade,' he screamed to his brother and rushed with it to the olive tree. But on reaching it he halted abruptly, and stood gazing into the distance as if he were seeing a vision. Then he suddenly turned to a freshly-dug crater at the foot of the tree and now, pale as death, he stared at a few pieces of half-rotten wood which lay exposed in the middle of the crater. He stumbled, grabbed the pieces and began to cry like a desperately unhappy child. He wailed and moaned repeating again and again, 'They have cheated me, they have cheated me, they have robbed me of my treasure!'

As he lifted the pieces of wood above his head, we could see that they were undoubtedly the counterparts of the broken crucifix we had just seen in the chapel.

3

By Caravan

I T took us several days to forget our gruesome experience
with Fortunato. Wallowing among the skulls and bones had
subdued us and our mood seemed to fit the endless emptiness
of the Peruvian coast. As we made our way south this melancholy
was wiped away by the beautiful old town of Arequipa, which
seen from afar, was a green oasis in an endlessly barren landscape.

Arequipa lies in a narrow green valley where every corner of
the rich volcanic earth brims over with many kinds of vegetables
and fruit such as figs, peaches, apricots, oranges and lemons.
The valley has a perfect Riviera climate and the sun seems to
shine eternally from an unbelievably blue sky.

The town, which was founded by the early Spanish settlers,
has preserved its colonial atmosphere perfectly. The majority of
the population are descendants of the Incas or the Spaniards, but
there is also a sprinkling of Asians and Europeans. We found
them delightful company and most helpful to visitors or new
settlers. We enjoyed bathing in the health-giving hot springs on
the outskirts of the town, or driving down the beautiful roads to
spend the day on the shores of the blue Pacific. The town has a
lovely cathedral built in the old Spanish style and a gay market
place where Aenne loved to do her shopping.

We were forced to stay in Arequipa for nearly two months
because the engine of our car had to be overhauled. I wanted it
to be right because we planned to go high over the roof of the
world to Pulcallpa and the jungles of the Amazon.

An accident to Graciela also delayed us. She had been showing
off on her little bicycle and had raced 'without hands' down the

19

steep road and crashed. She was unconscious and drenched in blood when I picked her up and carried her to a friend's house. Later her nose, which she had broken, became septic and had to be operated on. Since then Graciela has had a different face, for her nose which used to be narrow is now broad and does not seem to belong to her. But we were happy that she was well again and did not suffer any after-effects from her concussion.

When Graciela and the car were at last in good shape we left Arequipa. The engine purred happily as it pulled us up the steep pass in second gear. To our left towered the snow-clad peak of the volcano Misti and to the right the snow fields of the Pichu-Pichu sparkled in the sun. We met herds of llama, whose thick white wool blended perfectly with the scenery. At about fifteen thousand feet the long steep ascent ended and we came out on a gently undulating mountain plateau. Here the road ended and we followed a path until we reached a place where tracks suddenly fanned out in all directions. I had no idea which was the one that would take us to the nearest petrol station at Juliaca on Lake Titicaca, but I had somehow to find the right track because the wrong one would lead to disaster. We had only enough petrol left for a hundred and thirty miles, and as the temperature dropped to below freezing at night it was easy to imagine what might happen if I made the wrong choice and we got stuck hundreds of miles from human habitation. But my second sense as an old jungle vagabond, plus my usual luck, put us right and after driving on for two hours we saw an Esso sign which said '165 km. to Juliaca'.

We passed huge herds of wild Alpaca llamas, but our real thrill came when we spotted our first Vicuña deer. These lovely animals look a little like large European deer and have watery brown eyes and ears permanently at the alert. They take flight at the slightest noise, but I found their movements the most graceful of any animal I have ever seen. Their bodies are covered with fine soft wool of a reddish-brown colour, and on the breast and legs they have long white tufts of fur which give them a ragged gay appearance. They move in small herds of between nine and twelve animals and have survived only on the highest mountain plains of Peru, Bolivia and Chile. At one time they populated the Andes in great numbers and it was the privilege of the ruling Incas to hunt them. Later, after the Spanish Conquest, the warm soft wool of the Vicuña was popular in Spain and was so much in demand that the animals became almost extinct. Only now that they are under the protection of the State are their numbers slowly increasing again.

We expected to reach Lake Titicaca during the next day, and soon we saw a vast expanse of water stretching away into the distance. Unfortunately it was not the lake, but a vast plateau flooded by the recent heavy rain. Neither road nor track could be seen, and we had to drive on the top of a dam several inches below water-level. All I could do was to follow the telegraph poles and when they turned away from the dam as we approached a village we found ourselves in a ditch. Luckily, some villagers came up and helped us on to the road again and we were able to carry on to Lake Titicaca.

We spent several weeks exploring round the lake. Titicaca lies almost twelve thousand feet above sea-level and the mountains and meadows surrounding it are carpeted with a great variety of flowers. Most of the local people are direct descendants of the Aymara and Quechua Indians. They may be a little degenerate, but there is still much of the pride and greatness of their past about them. They are a reserved, introverted people and it is impossible to get to know them unless one speaks their language.

Most of the Indians live off their smallholdings, growing mainly potatoes, wheat and maize. They have simple clay houses which are ideally insulated to make the hot days and cold nights bearable. The fishermen use graceful, sturdy boats which they build themselves. On the whole, these Indians have kept much of the traditional skill of their forefathers; they weave beautiful blankets from llama-wool in the traditional designs and colours, and they are famous for their rattles made from the hard, dried shells of local fruits. On these are engraved minute letters and drawings depicting the legends of their ancestors. With their bright *ponchos*—cloaks—and amusing knitted pixie hats, they are a colourful and picturesque sight.

The villages and settlements beside the lake are far apart and the tracks that connect them are bad, as are the cobblestone village streets. On Sundays and holidays the inhabitants of these small communities trek for hours to go to church and afterwards enjoy themselves with drunken celebrations.

On Good Friday in 1953, we reached Taraco, a typically charming little town which has preserved not only its early colonial architecture, but also its old way of life. A Spanish church stands in the middle of the town opposite huge stone idols which grin down on the milling holiday crowds. The idols, worshipped for centuries by the Incas, had been moved to the town from their holy places several hundred years ago.

The large church could not hold the thousands of barefoot Indians from far and wide who came to attend the service. They knelt or squatted outside the church while Indian lay-priests, who had set up in competition, read their psalms and blessed the worshippers with water sprinkled out of brandy bottles. In return the preachers received eggs, potatoes, maize and fruit which were arranged around each of them like beautiful still-life pictures. When they had paid their contribution to the church, the Indians sold their remaining home-grown products, and invested the money in coca-leaves and brandy. By the early afternoon there was not a sober Indian in the town. They were still happily shouting and singing when they started on their long treks home.

Almost all the inhabitants in this region chewed coca-leaves. Under the influence of the cocaine they did not mind the thin air so troublesome to visitors and seemed to forget their poverty and misery. To the Quechua Indians coca-leaves are as important as bread is to us. When they go on journeys their most important piece of luggage is a little sack of these leaves. With the enjoyment of coca every other desire disappears. One feels beautifully detached and untouched by the problems of mind and body. As long as the effects of the drug last one feels no hunger, thirst or tiredness. Coca is not as harmful as marijuana but it has, no doubt, a degenerating effect.

One can buy these leaves anywhere in Peru in any quantity and almost every shop has sacks of them standing around. I tried chewing some of the leaves when I had toothache. At first the bitter taste was hardly bearable, but the toothache disappeared and soon I did not find the taste unpleasant. My problems dissolved and I could not

*The volcano Misti, near
Arequipa*

Inca mummy (see page 15)

understand how I could ever have worried about the outcome of the journey I had planned. I began to feel optimistic and pleased with life and my surroundings. I have since occasionally chewed the leaves and when it was a question of surmounting formidable difficulties, they have been of tremendous help to me. But I have always been on my guard; the stuff is undoubtedly habit forming.

We left Lake Titicaca, which was the most southerly part of our journey, to turn north and drive through the Andes towards the sources of the Amazon. The road led us through a fertile valley, which had small prosperous farms where slim eucalyptus trees grew in rich meadows, watered by the rushing stream that ran parallel to our route. Whenever we stopped in one of the small villages the people received us with friendly curiosity and we were given excellent meals for very little money in the village inns. As we drove on, the snow-capped mountains rose steeply from either side of the road which ran through the valley that formed the route of the Incas when they went to the formidable castle of Machu Picchu.

Machu Picchu means 'lost city', and it is in fact a lost city of the Incas which was discovered only in the year 1911. Its beautifully proportioned stone buildings and temples are still in good repair. The Spaniards never found this town which is hidden in a narrow valley leading to a pass that is usually engulfed in clouds or mist. As far as is known, Machu Picchu was never captured but died slowly when the freedom and pride of the Inca nation was destroyed. It is believed that the city was dedicated to the Sun God and that in its temples virgins were sacrificed to him.

Later, the road took a sharp turn and climbed even more steeply, first into the mist and then into the clouds. When we reached the summit, however, the sun broke through and we could see the endless plain gradually merging into the deep green sea of the jungle. Up here, more than thirteen thousand feet high, we were shivering from the cold, but down below the air was vibrating with heat and I was longing to fill my lungs with its heavy dampness. The combination of the light exhilarating air and the prospect of being again in the jungle gave me a feeling of exuberance and elation which made the twelve years of longing and waiting worth while. It seemed strange to me

c

now that during those years of waiting I could have feared an anticlimax when I at last returned to the jungle.

Eagerly we began the long descent into the steaming heat of the plain. Slowly the vegetation changed from lean grass to green bushes and soon there were ferns covering the ground. After a further few hours we reached the jungle. We discovered our first orchids, high up in the bare branches of some dead trees, and saw a poisonous snake ready to pounce on a baby howler monkey. The jungle was at its most typical. The stage was set like the first scene of a play but we did not yet know what was to follow.

On our right, the Madre de Dios, a rushing silver stream, followed the road for a long time. I was longing to get off the road and take a dugout into the interior, but the natives when I asked for a boat said that it was too near the rainy season to risk such an adventure. It was a dreadful disappointment to be so close to my beloved jungle, to smell and feel it, and yet to be unable to remain with it. Had I been alone no one would have held me back, but with the responsibility of a family, I decided not to take the risk.

A little sad, we returned to the mountains to continue our long journey due north to the sources of the Amazon. Just past Cuzco near the Urubamba river we came across some Inca burial places. There were twenty of them, small squat buildings made of large stones. Such burial places are the goal, even today, of adventurers who roam the lonely valleys in search of the gold and treasures which the Incas always buried with their dead.

The Indians who live in this region still follow many old customs. They wear a brightly coloured *poncho* and flat hat, which looks like a plate with fringe. We arrived at Paucartambo just as a wedding was taking place. The bride and groom and the guests were in their Sunday-best and the groom carried a lasso to catch his bride. There was a great deal of horse-play, lots of laughter and music. The head of the village, carrying a glittering silver staff, the sign of his high office, married the pair.

When important economic or other decisions have to be made in villages the men meet in an open field and the headman, carrying the silver staff, presides. After decisions have been taken the headman, who is usually the only person to speak Spanish, reports to the Government representative.

From Cuzco we drove on a beautiful but terrifying mountain road to La Oroya where we left the main route to visit the Tyrolean village of Oxapampa. We were now driving on the most dangerous road in Peru, one which we won't easily forget. At a village called Palca, what is known as the 'big skid' begins.

Here a control barrier is set across the road. A police officer explained to us with great gusto that on Sundays and Mondays only uphill traffic was allowed. It was very complicated, but in spite of the rules I was theoretically allowed to drive down from six o'clock on Sunday evening to eight o'clock on Monday morning. I was told with great emphasis that our vehicle was not the kind to do this trip. We hardly listened to the policeman's eloquent descriptions of the many ways we could come to grief, and started on our journey conscious of the fact that we had to be down by eight next morning.

As soon as we started we realised that the officer's florid descriptions were not unfounded. The road was little more than a mushy, slimy path with rocks rising vertically at one side and a drop of thousands of feet on the other. There were low tunnels and untidily overhanging rocks all along the route. When we started the air was brittle and fresh and the sky was covered with thousands of tiny sparkling stars; then came the mist. Soon we heard a splintering crash; an overhanging rock had taken off a corner of our roof. So as not to lose our hut I had to drive on the outer edge of the slippery road. I drove always with the door open to help me judge distances, praying for luck. And then, without warning, six lorries came towards me. They were carrying timber, but as their loads were only half the height of mine they did not have to fear the low tunnels and overhanging rocks. I squeezed to the outside edge. One, two, three. One after another the lorries passed with less than an inch to spare, and then as I was already drawing a deep sigh of relief the last lorry ripped open the side of my car. Aenne, Graciela and myself jumped out and stood paralysed, already imagining our beloved home crashing thousands of feet below. But somehow, although the car was pushed to the very extreme edge of the abyss, nothing happened and I was able to manoeuvre it inch by inch into the road again. By now our nerves were in such a state that we decided to wait for the light before continuing.

When light came and we saw the three thousand feet vertical drop from the place where we had had our collision, our stomachs turned and we wished we had not waited to see it. Another six hours of tortuous driving and we had reached the foot-hills of the Andes. Here the way led through thick jungle, broken at intervals by coffee, banana and orange plantations. We had reached the fringes of the 'fruit bowl' of Peru. The next day the valley of Oxapampa spread before us and we could see the little Tyrolean houses peeping out of the middle of the vast Peruvian pampas. We decided to take a long rest here before coping with the problem of the car which was scarcely holding together.

We had an introduction to a German settler called Johann Frantzen and called on him as soon as we arrived. He was the second generation to live in Oxapampa and he entertained us evening after evening with fascinating stories about his ancestors and local history. After a few days Johann and his charming wife asked us to stay in their home, an invitation which we gratefully accepted. Aenne, especially, enjoyed the luxury of a house, a real bed, a bath and some of the amenities of what we call civilisation. I, too, found it useful to have space to sort my photographs, write up my diary and rest.

Oxapampa really began, so Frantzen told me, in 1857 when three hundred Tyrolean immigrants battled their way over the Peruvian Andes and arrived in the valley of the Rio Pozuzo. The hundred and seventy who survived the journey cleared the jungle and founded the village of Pozuzo. Many decades passed before the outside world heard of them again. Meanwhile they had ploughed fields, improved their living conditions and married amongst each other.

There was, however, much malaria in the hot valley of Pozuzo so that at the beginning of the twentieth century a few of the young men set out to find a healthier and better place to live. After six days' journey they discovered a lovely valley, with

Mummy of fair-haired Inca (see page 17)

Fortunato digging up Inca mummies (see page 16)

Graciela with Inca skulls

The 'house on wheels' on the road to Oxapampa, with the author's wife in foreground

The balsa raft with Graciela on board

pastures of rich grass that stretched as far as the eye could see. This valley was called Oca by the natives and Oxapampa by the pioneers. They moved in. Maize, potatoes, coffee and rice grew there, and pigs, fowl and cattle thrived. Lima, the nearest town, was a week's journey away so there was not much sale for surplus produce, and prices for foodstuffs were kept ridiculously low. But everyone in the valley had more than enough and the prosperous farming community expanded rapidly.

Then the Peruvians built a road—the dangerous road by which we came. It was not only a dangerous road to drive on, it also turned out to be a danger to the community of Oxapampa. Before long the local people found it much more profitable to cut wood and work in the saw-mills or the box factories that came after the road had been built. The simple farmers of Oxapampa suddenly had their pockets full of silver coins and their wallets stuffed with notes. But the fields lay empty. Unfortunately they found the money worth very little. Meat, eggs and other food-stuffs had to come from the markets of Lima and were expensive by the time they reached Oxapampa. The money of the once-free peasants who were now labourers in the booming timber trade, flowed into the pockets of the tradesmen. Today the standard of living of the people is much lower than it used to be for they have plenty of money but not enough to eat. I saw them queueing at four in the morning for meat which is strictly rationed. Thus the new road has become the curse of the village. 'The old, quiet and prosperous times are gone,' Johann Frantzen said, but he was convinced they would come again. The timber rush was beginning to ebb; the best timber near the road had been felled and the saw-mill owners had earned their millions. Now they did not care if their machines were left to rust in the jungle, and the population which had increased to six thousand looked like being forced to return to the land.

Johann also told us about his father, First Mate Frantzen, who had left Germany in 1872 on a Finnish ship. He sailed all over the world and lived for a time in Hong Kong, eventually coming to Chile to work in a copper and silver mine. Then he decided to return to Germany, but his ship was wrecked and with some

of the crew Frantzen drifted for weeks on the open sea until they
hit land at the mouth of the Amazon. Here Frantzen was taken on
by a ship going up the Amazon and the Rio Negro as far as Manaos.

At that time the people of the town of Manaos were drunk
with fever of the rubber boom. Champagne flowed and real gold
nuggets tinkled in the pockets of the wild and rough-looking
adventurers who came up river to collect rubber from the unexplored jungle. On the map of South America there were still big
white patches indicating unexplored territory, and in the taverns
that Frantzen visited, exciting stories were told of mountains of
gold, jungle cities, blood-drinking Indians and powerful Amazons
who, like queen bees, destroyed their lovers after copulation.

Frantzen's imagination was inflamed by these stories and he
set out to find the sources of the Amazon. He became a hunter
and passionate nature lover and the wilderness became his home.
Later an Austrian and a Brazilian hermit joined him and together
they reached the mouth of the Rio Chuc Rurras where it flows
into the Palcazu. There they discovered a jungle clearing where
friendly Chucuito and Amoisha Indians lived. There were tapirs,
boars, deer, plenty of fish, wild fruit trees and many types of
monkeys and wild cats. This was exactly as Frantzen had
imagined paradise, and here the three adventurers built themselves huts and lived from hunting and fishing.

The Indians living near them became more and more trusting
and often stayed with the white men when they passed on their
hunting expeditions. Frantzen and his companions learned the
language of the Indians and had Indian mistresses. But although
they were well-liked and happy, they kept to themselves. After
several years they heard that only a ten days' trip away there
was a settlement of white people called Pozuzo. Frantzen went
to investigate but soon returned, with a wife, to his jungle home.
He changed his simple life and with free wood and cheap labour
he built a magnificent two-hundred-feet-long villa for his family.
His wife bore him two boys and a girl who were tall, blond and
healthy. They were sent to Germany to be educated and returned
to the jungle in 1914.

After a few years two more families from Pozuzo settled in

the paradise of Chuc Rurras and a community of farms grew up. Frantzen died in 1916 and his wife in 1939. Johann Frantzen, our host, had come to Oxapampa but his brother was still living with his family in the old parental home. We decided to visit him.

Chuc Rurras was in the direction of the Amazon valley, six days from Oxapampa. I was happy as a child to be in the jungle again and Aenne was spellbound by its wild magic, its luscious vegetation and wealth of animal life as we made our way along a narrow overgrown path. Graciela, too, was blissfully happy for everything was exactly as she had imagined it. On the way we surprised huge hordes of howler monkeys which protested so loudly at our presence that we could hardly hear ourselves talk. The whole jungle seemed to shudder and vibrate.

Unfortunately Johann developed a most painful attack of rheumatism and we had to pitch our first camp earlier than we had hoped. When I went to cut branches to support the palm leaf roof, which we were erecting to give us protection from the sun, I came across some very large jaguar tracks. But Johann was too occupied with his own troubles to be bothered with them.

I did not sleep well that night and woke with a feeling that we had a dangerous visitor. I did not know if I was still dreaming, but when I opened my eyes I saw a huge jaguar slinking past me in the light of the fire. Taking a glowing piece of wood from the fire I threw it and the beast disappeared. Johann only grunted when I tried to wake him. Next morning I showed him the jaguar tracks in the white ashes of the fire, but all he said was, 'You are too thin, Alfred, the jaguar has better taste than that.' He warned us that jaguars often follow people for many days and nights and in this he was only too right because we accidentally took an unwelcome visitor with us to Chuc Rurras.

Our reception at the urban and palatial villa in Chuc Rurras was enthusiastic. Visitors rarely come to this lonely paradise, so everyone took a few days' holiday to celebrate our arrival. When they returned to their cattle on the fertile pampas, they found the carcases of several young oxen waiting for them. There was no doubt that this was the work of our jaguar which followed us for five days. Johann and I felt responsible and determined to destroy the brute with the help of Johann's son.

We could expect no direct help from the Indians. They believe that the souls of their chiefs and medicine-men survive in the bodies of jaguars so that they will never kill one, however much damage it does. They seem to have no objection to others doing the killing, however, particularly if the late chief has not been very popular; on this occasion, they were quite happy to think that their enemy would be destroyed without their consciences being troubled.

We took six dogs to help us find the animal and hacked our way through the thick jungle with knives and hatchets. After some time I noticed something moving behind the thick trunk of a tree. Before I knew what had happened a huge jaguar had leapt from behind it straight on to one of our dogs. Jaguars are mad about dogs' meat and this one was no exception. Johann's son, who did not want to lose one of his best dogs, jumped on top of the fighting beast. He clamped the jaguar's soft waist tightly between his knees and pressed its head to the ground by the ears screaming to me 'pull out your knife and let him have it'. I snatched up the knife, grabbed Johann's son's elbow which was covering the jaguar's heart, and struck. It had all happened within seconds and the brute lay dying at our feet. The dog was badly mauled but the Frantzens nursed it back to perfect health.

The Indian tribes around Chuc Rurras still live very much as they had twenty years ago when Frantzen's father and his companions settled in the district. The European family had been completely accepted as neighbours by the Indians and the relationship between the settlers and the primitive but proud Indians, though not intimate, was good; it was based on matter-of-fact neighbourliness and mutual respect.

Aenne and Graciela were curious to meet some of the natives in their primitive settlements so I persuaded Johann to take us on a short trip to one or two of the tribes.

We travelled for two days through the thick jungle and eventually came to a clearing littered with the remains of many fires. On the edge of the clearing we could just see the entrances of small windowless huts made of plaited palm-leaves. The roofs slanted backwards until they almost touched the ground and there was nothing inside the huts except a fireplace near the door and some pots and pans scattered about. The natives slept in hammocks which were tied to wooden poles and were rolled up during the day. They were nice-looking people. The men had elaborate and well-kept hair styles and many of them were carefully painted with intricate designs. The young girls were pretty with good figures and wonderful breasts. We especially admired their erect, floating, liquid walk which was the result of carrying practically everything on their heads. Many of the old people looked hideous, especially when they wore such ill-assorted bits of Western clothing as a hat full of holes or a pair of underpants with the seat torn out. One old woman wore a man's shirt with her breasts hanging out.

The fact that so many of these natives were dressed in bits and pieces of Western clothing was a great disappointment for Aenne when she met her first primitives. I had never really warned her that the missionaries believed that they could only introduce the natives to God after their shameless nakedness was hidden and in so doing spoiled the beauty of Indian life. I had forgotten about it, probably because I considered these garments entirely superficial. An apparently unlimited amount of clothes was continuously distributed, free of charge, by the missionaries and found their way to some of the most remote tribes where they were not always worn in the spirit in which they were given. An Indian girl might wear a man's vest and burst open the top buttons with her shapely protruding breasts. Below the waist she would be covered only by a G-string. Sometimes these rags were used for warmth at night, or for protection against insects and thorns, and at other times with traditional war-paint and feathers. But these signs of civilisation affect the Indian way of life and customs very little.

The village chief of the natives we visited was called the *Curaca* and he greeted Johann in a friendly and respectful manner. His many wives, ranging from a girl of eleven to an old lady of sixty-five who was a great-great-grandmother, followed at a distance. There was not a piece of Western dress to be found on this most impressive grey-haired old man. As a sign of office and dignity he wore a long coloured chain made of dried fruits which stretched from his neck to his thighs. Around his arms he had feather ornaments and his hair was trimmed short in a sort of pageboy cut. Otherwise he wore nothing but a G-string. His chest, back and thighs were painted in red and white patterns, and he carried a beautifully carved stave adorned with rows of animal teeth and red, black and white feathers.

The *Curaca* took us to see the *Brujo*—the medicine-man—the second most important man in the tribe. He also wore no European garments, but the paint on his dark naked body was far more ornate than that of the *Curaca*. The *Brujo* was busy healing a sick man. The patient was lying on a beautifully woven palm leaf mat and was a pathetic-looking skeleton. He was almost certainly suffering from dysentery and to effect a cure the medicine-man, who knew this ailment as one of the most common in these parts, went through the antics handed down from generation to generation. He cooked tobacco leaves and made the patient drink the concentrated juice. Then he sucked the ailing stomach of the patient to extract the evil spirits and murmured all sorts of magic formulae.

Since nothing very startling seemed to happen and the *Brujo* wanted to impress us, he sent the relatives of the sick man to find a particular bone. While we were waiting, the *Brujo* blew tobacco smoke over the patient and danced round him. When the relatives returned without the bone they were beaten with a club and chased into the woods to make a further search. Johann told me that even if a satisfactory bone was found and the patient still did not recover, the *Brujo* would quite likely blame one of the relatives and have him killed.

A *Brujo* will usually try to blame others for his own failures, but if he overdoes it the tribe will lose faith in him and chase him out or poison him. In most tribes the chief sees that the *Brujo* does not get too tyrannical. Although he is feared and respected, a *Brujo's* reputation is always at stake and he can never rest on his laurels. He is always busy inventing new cures and magic formulae to maintain his reputation.

We did not wait until the right bones were found, but we watched the *Brujo* concocting medicines out of frogs, dead mice and all sorts of roots and herbs. If anybody had told me then that a few weeks later I would have been desperate enough to entrust the life of my little daughter to such a medicine-man, I would have laughed at him.

The whole life of the Indians, their relationship with each other, and their actions are largely governed by their belief in good and evil spirits. The ways of keeping these spirits happy vary. In most of the tribes the spirits of the dead are believed to live on in the shapes of certain animals and continue their relationships of love and hate with each other and with those still alive. The art of clairvoyance is taken seriously and every tribe has its experts who are consulted whenever important decisions have to be made. One way of telling the future in this region is to mix coca-leaves with lime and a tree-bark called chamayo, chew the mixture, spit it into your hand, shake it well three times, open your hand and then interpret the patterns of the juice.

We saw this done at Chuc Rurras when Johann's brother was clearing a path through a thick part of the jungle with the help of some local Indians and I accompanied them. We had arranged to meet another party cutting their way through from the other side. When evening came and there was no sign of the other party who carried all our rations, the Indians of Johann's brother's group became restive and worried. They decided to ask their expert clairvoyant for help. He took coca-leaves, bark and lime and went through the ceremony of chewing and spitting the juice into his hand. He predicted that the other party would never reach us and suggested we stop work immediately and force our way through the jungle. Before nightfall, he said, we would meet the other party of eight men. One of the eight men would have an injured leg and another a hurt back. I was doubtful about heeding this advice, but the Indians were determined so we forced our way on through the thicket. We were glad we did, because three or four hours later we met the other party and everything was exactly as it had been foretold. One man had injured his leg and another had a badly-strained back.

A Quechua Indian called Martin, who worked on the Frantzen's farm, specialised in telling the future from the smoke of his cigar. One day we heard the high pitched whining of a *lancha*'s siren. Everybody ran towards the river because it was not often that a boat reached this deserted stretch of the river. Martin watched the smoke of his cigar and predicted that the *lancha* would not arrive that day. No one believed him since it was the custom that the *lancha* always sounded its siren two bends before it reached Chuc Rurras. The *lancha* did not come, but long after sundown its crew came trudging through the jungle. They told us that a large floating palm tree had pierced the bottom of their boat and they had had to finish their journey on foot.

Every morning, when looking out of our bedroom window at Chuc Rurras, I had been fascinated by a red mountain rising out of the endless jungle. Thick green growth covered its lower slopes and the top was made up of rocks which glittered in the evening sun in many colours ranging from yellow to purple. When I asked Johann about it he said it was almost three thousand feet high and, as far as he knew, it had never been climbed. The Amuesha Indians called it the Miraz Mountain—the lightning mountain—and believed that no one could climb it and return alive. They said there was a lake on top and on it was a raft where a horde of red monkeys lived. These were the reincarnations of the dead and resented any disturbance from the living.

I could not understand how Johann could have lived all his life looking at this beautiful mountain without ever having tried to climb it. Now was the time, I told him, and I was so insistent that I persuaded him to climb it with me.

So Johann, his brother, myself and four Indians started off to conquer the Miraz Mountain. For two days we paddled up river in a dugout and then continued on foot. As soon as we reached the mountain the Indians became reluctant to carry on. Every hour or so one of them would halt and refuse to move any further, talking of the big red monkeys which would surely kill us. The higher we got the more persistent their complaints became. In the end the Indians would only continue if we promised to be very quiet so that we would not be noticed by the monkeys.

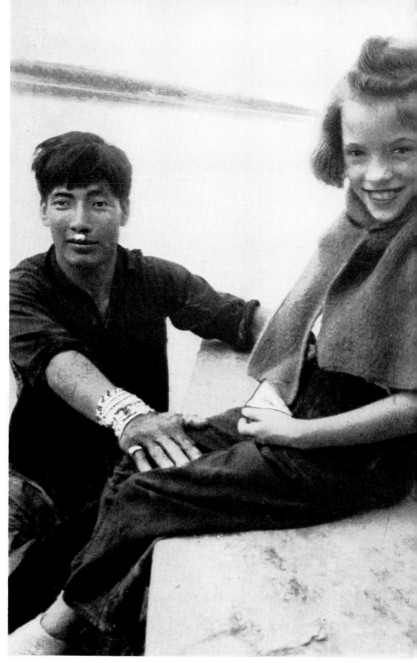

Graciela and the medicine-man (see page 40)

Two Indian women awaiting the result of the medicine-man's skill

The beginning of the Amazon: the confluence of the Ucayali and the Marañon

About a thousand feet below the top they stopped altogether. So we asked them to wait for us and continued on our own.

We had now left the jungle and were climbing over bright red sandstone. The sudden quiet after the accustomed jungle noises subdued us and we climbed on in silence. When we reached the summit we found a lake which seemed to cover the entire plateau. In the middle there was a bright red completely flat island washed over, here and there, by the water of the lake. The sun caught the glittering wet stone and reflected it like flashes of lightning.

We lit a fire to show the Indians that we had reached the top without being harmed by ghosts and that they could safely join us. When they did not come we fired some shots to draw their attention, but all we saw was four little figures stampeding out of sight. We caught up with them several hours later and they would hardly believe us when we told them that we had not been harmed by red monkeys or ghosts.

Back in Oxapampa it rained all the time and we spent many evenings sitting around the long, brightly scrubbed table in Johann's beautiful house. We heard stories of past feuds and battles with the natives and of the struggles of the first settlers. There was always talk about gold. Anything and everything about gold fascinated these people and they never tired of talking about it, nor did they ever give up hope of finding it.

There was no doubt that there had been a lot of gold in this region. The Incas had mined there and their most beautiful ornaments were made of gold. Johann's father had amassed most of his riches by washing gold and his sons had crossed the jungle many times in search of new sources. The Indians, although quite open and trusting in every other matter, become cunningly secretive and vicious where gold is mentioned.

About forty years ago an Indian woman who still lives near Oxapampa, used regularly to return to her home from the jungle carrying small sacks of pure gold nuggets. She never gave anyone the slightest hint where she found them. The whole community went crazy with curiosity and many prospectors tried to follow her trail to discover the secret. No one succeeded. Then a brash young German prospector arrived and immediately began to court the girl. Although she was flattered and accepted his attentions with pleasure and enthusiasm, he never learned her secret. In desperation he decided to live with her, but even then she would not tell him where she found the gold. She made a point of fetching the nuggets when he was away selling the previous haul. They had several children but he never married her because he knew that not even marriage would make her reveal the secret.

Eventually we had to say goodbye to the generous and charming Frantzens. Looking back, I realise that staying with this straightforward and practical family who had acclimatised themselves so completely to jungle life and got so much out of it, was the best introduction to the jungle that Graciela and Aenne could have had.

We had to take the skid road back to Tarma, but this time we drove during the day and had the right of way. From Tarma our road led us to Cerro de Pasco, one of the highest ore mines in South America. We had to use snow chains through the wonderful mountain ranges and later through the delightful villages on the shores of the Lago de Junin. Here we left the high mountains of Peru for good and took the steep road through Huánuco down to the plains of the Amazon. At Tingo Maria we at last entered the jungle which was to be our home for thousands of miles during the next three years. We now had only another hundred and fifty miles to go by car, but this last lap was on the infamous 'Soap Road'. Every thirty miles along it there was a hut with a caretaker who stopped all traffic as soon as there was any sign of rain. There are no stones in the Amazon valley, so the road had no foundations and when it rained cars slithered about on it as if on soft soap. The caretaker at the first hut we came to showed us a huge boulder and explained that this was the last stone we would see for a long time.

After three days on the 'Soap Road' we reached the little town of Pucallpa on the River Ucayali, the starting point of our 'real' journey.

4

Our New Home

AT last we were at the end of all passable roads or even
mule tracks. Before us lay the endless jungle along the
banks of the River Ucayali, one of the many tributaries
of the Amazon. My plan was to travel by balsa raft across South
America, until I reached the Atlantic.

But it was not so easy to find these balsa logs. I was told there
were none left within fourteen days' journey. The new motor-way
which had been built to this distant point had opened the country
to the timber merchants who had cut down all the balsa trees.

I spent the next few weeks searching the river banks for any
balsa trees which the rainy season might have floated down. I
managed to collect nine, each with a minimum diameter of four
feet. Cocama Indians helped me transform these nine rough
pieces of timber into a seaworthy raft. They were very good raft
builders with a skill passed on from generation to generation for
many hundreds of years. The balsa logs were bound together with
lianas, which will stand a greater stress than steel, and then
wedged with hardwoods. This perfect piece of workmanship and
construction was to keep us afloat for several years, withstanding
tropical storms, rapids and collisions.

I had designed the hut on our car chassis in such a way that it
could be lifted off by loosening only six screws. Now I transferred
it to the raft where it took up less than half the available area.
On most of the remaining space I built a kind of loggia enclosed
in fine wire-netting; this was to be our sitting-room and kitchen
for the next few years. The hut served as our bedroom, giving
protection for the nights.

A raft of this size would normally need two strong men to navigate it. Since I was alone there was nothing left for me to do but to buy a small motor-boat so that I could tow the raft to the middle of the stream or manoeuvre it away from the many hazardous places along the river bank if I ran into difficulties. I managed to get an old motor-boat hull at a nearby saw-mill and a simple eight horse-power American motor, originally designed to drive a dynamo, which I adapted to drive the boat's propeller. Later, when navigating the many rapids of the Rio Negro and the Orinoco, and riding out sudden tropical storms, our survival depended entirely on this little motor and the screw it turned.

I bartered away the car chassis to an Indian for forty bottles of schnapps. He felt that this contraption, placed like a monument in front of his hut, would enhance his standing.

At two o'clock on 16 June 1953, we were at last ready to depart. Slowly our motor-boat pulled the heavy raft into midstream. Nearly all the inhabitants of Pucallpa assembled on the river bank to watch us leave and we could hear snatches of their conversation. There were arguments as to how far we might get with our contraption, speculations as to what would happen to us when we reached the rapids and graphic descriptions of mighty tropical storms which had wrecked at least a dozen rafts manned by skilful Indians.

We sailed without incident and were soon floating happily downstream on the next leg of our long journey.

Shortly before sunset I thought it was time to prepare for our first landing. Spotting a well-protected white sandbank, I jumped into the motor-boat and ran on to it at full speed. There was nothing wrong with this procedure since the boat had only a one-foot draught and I expected the raft to follow it nicely on to the sands. But the swift current of the river upset my plans. Turning round on its own axis the raft swept past the sandbank, pulling the motor-boat free and leaving me literally high and dry on the sandbank. I leapt into the water trying to stop the heavy raft and motor-boat from running away, but it was hopeless. I just managed to scramble on to the raft where

I collapsed on the verandah to reflect on our difficult position.

We could not, I realised, drift down the Amazon for ever, exposed to the whims of the mighty river. Darkness had come very suddenly for there is practically no twilight in this latitude and we floated on in the black of the night. From time to time we could hear a deep, eerie rushing sound from the giant jungle trees which had been uprooted and now overhung the steep river banks and trailed spiky branches above the rushing water. These uprooted trees—called *palasadas* by the natives—are the terror of the Amazon and we had been warned about them in Pucallpa. There was always the danger that the raft would be stopped by these overhanging trees and then capsised by the pressure of the water.

To avoid the palasadas I jumped into the motor-boat and towed the raft out into the stream. An hour later when the moon came up we found ourselves drifting peacefully in the middle of the river. Before long a counter-current caught us on a bend and pushed us gently on to a sandbank. It was as easy as that and we were very pleased to be able to relax on the firm sandbank in the cool moonlit night. I stopped worrying about the future. I could see that it was no use fighting the river and the heavy raft with my physical strength and an eight horse-powered motor. Only skill could help me and this I would only acquire through experience.

We could not continue our journey next morning as our little Graciela was tossing and turning in her bunk with a high temperature caused by a serious attack of tonsilitis. I had not had enough money to equip a proper medicine chest and had only one phial of penicillin left. I gave her an injection and she went to sleep peacefully so that we thought our troubles were over. By evening she seemed to have made a remarkable recovery but during the night she again became delirious. The effect of the penicillin had worn off and I had no more. Her tonsils were now so swollen that I feared she would suffocate. She had difficulty in breathing and her lungs laboured to force the air through the tiny opening still left in her throat.

Aenne occupied herself massaging Graciela's neck with fat

D

and putting cold compresses on her head and giving her aspirin. This way she managed to keep calm. All I could do was sit and watch my little girl struggle for life. It was torture. I accused myself of gross selfishness for exposing her immature and vulnerable little body to the hazards of primitive life. I suddenly realised that although it was easy for me to abjure civilisation and worship the primitive jungle life, I had little right to deny my child the advantages of civilisation which were her birthright. I knew that Graciela's illness had reached such a critical stage that only drastic action by a doctor could save her life. How I yearned for civilisation!

I was so deeply immersed in my thoughts that I did not notice the Indian canoe which had tied up to our raft until I saw two inquisitive eyes peering through the mosquito wire. I went out and saw a man and woman sitting in a dugout and by the symmetrical pattern woven into their clothes I recognised them as Chami Indians. I talked to them in Spanish, but they could not understand, so by signs I invited the man on to the raft. I showed him Graciela, put my hands together as if in prayer and looked him deep in the eyes. He seemed to understand that I needed his help. He quickly returned to his boat and raced downstream to the other side of the river bank. I wondered anxiously what he was going to do, but was feeling a little calmer now that I knew that at least something was happening. I half hoped that the Indian knew of some ancient remedy to cure my daughter.

In the meantime Aenne kept busy preparing new compresses soaked in vinegar. After several hours, which seemed like days, without improvement of Graciela's condition, the Indian dugout returned. Another Indian now squatted at the helm and he looked sympathetic and intelligent. On his wrists were heavy silver rings beautifully inlaid with jaguar's teeth and a silver ring pierced his nose. By the way he examined Graciela I was sure he was the tribal medicine-man.

He left but soon came back carrying a dead snake in one hand and some roots, herbs and leaves in the other. He made a small fire on the sandbank and then pounded the herbs and roots into a mash and threw them into a beautifully decorated bowl of boiling water. He left this until the water had almost evaporated and a thick sticky liquid remained. He now skinned the snake to get the thick layer of fat which covered its flesh. This he heated in another bowl until it melted into a thin oil. When all the sifting, mixing and stirring was done the medicine-man opened Graciela's mouth with a firm but gentle touch, dipped a long bird's feather into the thick broth and painted her throat and tonsils with quick practised skill. Then he dipped large leaves into the melted snake's fat and tied them with a thin liana thread around her neck.

Drawing a handful of tobacco leaves from a little bag, he rolled himself a large cigar, lit it, and blew thick clouds of smoke over Graciela, mumbling magic words and formulae at the same time. This was to drive the sickness from her body. All afternoon he painted her throat and put leaves round her neck and blew smoke over her. Then as evening came he departed.

All through that night Aenne and I sat by Graciela's side tortured by doubts. Were we mad to have allowed a wild Indian medicine-man to try his magic tricks on our sick child? Should we take her back in the motor-boat to Pucallpa, or try to have her carried there on a stretcher? Why had we ever taken her on this dangerous voyage? Why had we not stayed in Caracas and brought her up properly in civilised surroundings? We blamed ourselves like this all night, the longest and most gruelling night of our lives. Whatever happened we meant to give up our trip. Without Graciela we would not feel like going on, and should she recover we could not take this kind of risk again.

As the sun rose our daughter fell into a deep sleep, her breath became even and her flushed face took on a natural colour. The medicine-man came back. He seemed very pleased and performed a little war dance. It might have been simply for the joy of seeing Graciela so much better, or it could have been a ritual dance to thank the spirits for curing our daughter. It was a very gentle and quiet sort of dance and when it was finished he departed without waking the child.

When Graciela awoke next morning she had only one desire: to get out of bed. We inspected her throat and took her temperature and found everything normal, but we felt we must keep her lying down. After all, only a few hours before she had been on the brink of death. By using all my powers of persuasion and whatever fatherly authority I could muster, I managed to keep her in bed until eleven o'clock. Then I gave up and when the medicine-man came back, she was sitting happily on the shady side of the boat painting. The Indian grinned from ear to ear, patted her knee with his beringed hand in a fatherly way and allowed himself to be admired by the members of the tribe whom he had brought along. The success he had had with the little white patient had enhanced his standing with his tribe immensely.

In spite of the previous night's resolutions we continued our journey early next morning. The river was still and the air warm and humid as we drifted peacefully past endless miles of jungle. Every few hours we would spot a palm-leaf hut and I would set out in the motor-boat to investigate and talk to the natives. I usually returned with something to eat: oranges, lemons or bananas.

There are supposed to be fifty-eight kinds of banana, from the tiny Platano de Oro—the golden banana—which never gets larger than three inches, to the green cooking banana which weighs up to two pounds. The colours can be yellow, red, blue and violet. The taste of the many varieties is amazingly different. The Platano—the apple-banana—tastes exactly like a sweet-sour apple of which the most delicate in flavour is a red variety. The large green bananas are usually eaten cooked like potatoes or sliced and deep-fried like chips. That was Graciela's favourite dish and Aenne used to complain that her major occupation during the journey was frying banana chips.

For her cooking, Aenne used the same petrol pressure cooker that she had used in the car caravan. Here, in the shade of the palm roof of our loggia, cooking was a more pleasant task. Washing-up was done from one of the balsa logs, and many a plate, spoon and cup was taken from us by the Amazon. When doing her laundry, Aenne, too, had a constant battle with the soap for which the deep waters of the river seemed to have a magnetic attraction.

This was the dry season and all sorts of beautiful sandbanks had come to the surface. Fish were abundant, and we passed many Indians drawing their nets and pulling in great varieties. We had fish for almost every meal. Graciela was especially fond of the little palomitas—a small fish which is as flat as our plaice, but swims thin side up. My wife had no menu problems since Graciela demanded bananas or palomitas for every meal. We hardly remembered what bread tasted like and did not miss it.

The Amazon has something like fifty different edible varieties of fish. The large zungarro—called a tiger-fish because its back is striped like that of a tiger—makes a wonderful soup, when cooked with salt and garlic, which is hardly distinguishable from good chicken broth. There is also a pretty coloured fish with bright red salmon-like flesh which tastes, when baked, like tender Wiener Schnitzel. Whenever we met natives they gave us fish, for there was so much about at that time of the year (June and July) that the fishermen hardly knew what to do with their catch. We usually tied up for the night near a hut or settlement for company. It was fun being with the gay and inquisitive natives. The appearance of three blond Europeans, including a lively little girl, was not an everyday occurrence for them. Anyone who says there is no hospitality left in the world should travel down the tributaries of the Amazon. He would soon revise his opinion.

As we drifted on, black mudbanks appeared by the yellow ones. Huge canoes overtook us laden with whole families from grandmother to babes in arms and carrying household goods, dogs, chickens and parrots; all were talking and laughing and would wave to us in good humour. These people were nomadic farmers in search of a suitable mudbank where they could build a hut of palm-leaves and plant rice. Such a mudbank, depending on its size, could yield up to fifty tons of rice on which the family would live in their village during the rainy season. Until the rice was ready to be harvested, the Indians lived almost entirely on fish.

The only thing which marred our leisurely trip down the beautiful stretch of the Ucayali river was an epidemic of whoop-

ing cough. We thanked God that we had had Graciela inoculated
before we left, but it was heartbreaking to watch a boat-load of
children half suffocating from coughing. We could hear the
wheezing, retching and coughing chorus long before a boat came
into sight and we continued to hear these heart-rending sounds
long after it disappeared. We could do nothing to help the unfortunate children as we had not been able to afford more than
basic medical supplies.

The Rio Ucayali wound itself through the thick jungle like a
giant snake. Sometimes its bends were so wide that we drifted
through them for several days only to be greeted by an Indian
to whom we had said goodbye a day or two earlier at a place only
half-an-hour's trek away by land. Whenever I consulted my
map to check our progress I found that we had hardly moved
and it seemed to us as if we were on a journey without end.

Even during the dry season it rained and became chilly for a
couple of days when the moon changed. The clouds would hang
like fog over the river and everything grew silent and paralysed.
The only life seemed to be in the water where the big fishes
terrorised the little ones into leaping to the surface.

It was at this time we were adopted by bufeos, fishlike mam-
mals which noisily puffed air from their lungs as they accompanied our raft for days. Bufeos are sacred to the natives who
believe that each one carries the spirit of a dead man. Although
quite harmless, these inquisitive creatures were up to twenty
feet long and made us uncomfortable about Graciela who was
always rushing fearlessly round the raft at hair-raising speeds
and in danger of falling into the water.

All along the river the hoarse shriekings of the ara parrots
could be heard from the tops of the giant jungle trees. We were
always hearing, too, the deep resonant call of the chorus leader
of the howler monkeys which kept on until an entire pack joined
in, filling the air with an ear-splitting, terrifying noise. This
uproar lasted for only a few minutes and the stillness that
followed made all the other jungle noises seem the more subtle
and mysterious. Mud, sandbanks, fallen trees, currents and the
ever-changing level of the river made tying-up at nights a

problem. One morning we found ourselves grounded high and dry on a sandbank. This time we were saved by an Indian of the Cocamilla tribe who lived nearby and who found twenty of his tribal brothers to lever us back into the water with long hardwood poles. Without this assistance we would have had to wait for at least eight months for the river to rise sufficiently to refloat us. From then on I made sure that we had at least three feet of water beneath us during the night and that we were not anchored over a hollow in the river-bed which would become a puddle surrounded by sand if the water-level fell. Sometimes large sandbanks criss-crossed by long navigable channels grew out of the river during the night. When we were caught on one of these sandbanks it was difficult to decide which channel was suitable for the raft.

On one occasion I allowed the raft to drift through a three-hundred-feet-broad channel, rather than make a long detour round the sandbank. As we went along the water became shallower while the current became faster. I was horrified, but before I had a chance to do anything about it we ran aground. I jumped out and tried to free the raft, but I was helpless against the power of the fast-moving current. It seemed that without the help of another twenty natives we would be imprisoned until the rainy season refloated us. But on a barren sandbank at the dead end of a canal leading to nowhere it was unlikely that anyone would come our way. We had to act quickly. Aenne and Graciela joined me in the water and together we pushed and heaved. But the raft would not move; in desperation I hitched up the motor-boat, set it at full speed ahead, jumped out and pushed it in the right direction. Inch by inch we fought our way upstream to a greater depth. There was no time to think of the poisonous thornback fish which might have been lurking at just such a place. It took us two hours to get back to the main canal from which we had diverged in less than ten minutes.

A few hours later when we were again drifting down the silent and peaceful river the adventure seemed as unreal as if we had seen it in a cinema. Lying in the shade of our mosquito-proof verandah, drifting through the damp, rich jungle and listening to its mysterious sounds, we felt as if the vast river was endless and that we would continue to drift on like this for ever.

Less than two weeks after our departure from Pucallpa we reached Contamana, the seat of the Government and the capital of the province. Contamana consisted of one single two-mile-long street. There was only one side of the street left, the houses on the other side having been torn away by the rushing flood waters of the river during the previous rainy season. Like the sandbanks and mudbanks, the river often changed its course without warning and large villages which once lay on its banks were often left ten to fifteen miles away in the middle of the jungle. This eccentric behaviour made our maps useless.

The wife of the American missionary in Contamana invited us to a wonderful dinner where we drank iced water from brightly coloured aluminium beakers, ate bread with real American tinned butter, and enjoyed especially the sweet made of flour, that followed. Graciela loved this visit, especially the meal, and was thrilled by the novelty and the change. But Aenne and I felt tense and uncomfortable at being dropped so suddenly into a civilised home. We hardly dared to talk loudly or tread firmly on the carpeted floor, and kept warning Graciela not to upset things. As I sat in the comfortable easy chair I felt like a rabbit caught in a trap and my eyes were hypnotised by the glare of the bright electric light bulb. I felt more naked than an Indian.

Nearly all of the missionaries on the Ucayali and Amazon come from America and have a good life. Their monthly dollar cheques allow them pleasures beyond the dreams of the natives. With love and sincerity and with the help of their dollar cheques, they try to entice the Indians to their little wooden churches. As long as there is some material reward, most Indians will go to church and watch with some surprise and considerable interest the antics of the white folk trying to teach them a new belief. But they seldom understand the teaching. A Catholic bishop, in the deep interior of South America, once told me, 'Don Alfredo, stay with us and become a missionary. You manage to do more with these Indians in two weeks than we can in a lifetime.'

We stayed in Contamana for four days, but received only this one invitation to dinner. I feel sure it was because we had not gone to a service at the little wooden church. Perhaps this was not very nice of us as the church was filled with people that evening, waiting to take a good look at the white visitors who had arrived on the strange raft.

From Contamana to the next provincial capital, or rather a village called Orellana, we made good time and covered the quite appreciable distance in five days of drifting. We felt it was high time that our coffers were replenished—I simply had to make some money. Before we left I had equipped the raft with a small photographic laboratory where I could even make enlargements. The electric current I took from my old car battery. I was lucky at Orellana. We arrived on the *dia de los maestros*—the day of the teachers—in the local school. This school had a hundred pupils and was financed by the Peruvian Government. The headmaster was delighted when I offered to give the pupils a talk about the mountain Indians of Peru. After the lecture, to which teachers and pupils listened in rapt attention, I had them all lined up in the courtyard of the school and, climbing the flagpole, took a photograph of the whole group. There were over a hundred of them and for a small payment which I graciously accepted, each one of them received a photograph as a memento of the great occasion of our visit. Now the bottom, at least, of our little tin savings bank was again covered with shiny pieces of money.

After we left Orellana the swift current of the Ucayali took us still deeper into the jungle. Our next destination was the village called 2 de Mayo. We had been expecting to reach it any day, but since we had not seen a living soul en route we had no idea how far we had to go. I tried to follow our progress on the map, but this was hopeless and I ended by tearing it to bits. At last we met two Indians in a canoe who told us that we had passed the village of 2 de Mayo a long way back. Years ago it had been situated on the river bank, but now it could only be reached by walking for several hours along a jungle track. After the fishermen had explained this to us in great detail they gave us some large fish and we drifted on still further into the un-inhabited wilderness.

For the next few weeks it seemed as if we were the only human beings in a vast stretch of wild, prolific nature. Game had become much more plentiful and as the animals had had no previous experience of human beings they were extraordinarily tame. The bufeos became even more cheeky and played around us the whole day long. They rubbed their heavy bodies against the raft, making it creak and shudder as they tried to scrape off some of the parasites which live on their hides. At the sight of us the howler monkeys commenced their chorus and once a huge, black-white-and-red bird followed us, braying above us like a donkey. We could now add wild duck, hare and deer to our regular menu. At many places we discovered herons, often in groups of many hundreds. But it was only at night when our raft was securely anchored by the banks of the river and we were resting in our hammocks on the verandah that the jungle really came to life.

As soon as the sun disappeared below the horizon, a strange humming sound began which quickly increased until it sounded like hundreds of aeroplanes taking off from a nearby airfield. This sound, gaining strength from minute to minute, came from millions of mosquitos who wait for dusk before venturing on their nightly assaults. Any white person overtaken by these swarms would be pitifully mutilated.

Now and then a shudder would run down our spines when a swarm of mosquitos, in a mass so thick that we could no longer see out, suddenly settled on the wire mesh. This scourge is the reason why the jungle paradise of the upper Ucayali has been avoided by men. The few Indians who live there rub their bodies with a fluid made of certain roots, which smells so frightful that even the mosquitos flee in terror from it. On the raft we could enjoy the security of our wire enclosed verandah and could lay around on the deck or rest in our hammocks in perfect peace.

In most places, the Rio Ucayali has two completely different river banks. One is low with wide sandbanks; the other, where the swift current has eaten deeper into the jungle, is steep and rugged. In the dry season the river falls anything up to thirty feet below the level of the banks and the stillness of the day is often broken by the thunderous noise of a huge jungle tree crashing down the crumbling slopes. These fallen trees form the feared *palasadas* and woe to any craft that gets sucked into their tangled branches.

Sometimes these trees float on the water, their roots still anchored to the bank. Their smooth trunks and tousled heads swing regularly to and fro in the current like the pendulum of a clock. Here in the jungle amid the most forceful and prolific of Nature's creations even dead objects seem lifelike. There is an ever-present pulsating movement, change is followed by change, and stillness by upheaval. From the sunny languid peace of a hot day a thunderstorm swiftly breaks, uprooting, whipping and destroying all in its path. The rain comes down from the black clouds in an opaque mass and the river banks disappear from sight and one is lost in water. Then suddenly the sun breaks through again, engulfing everything in thick oppressive heat.

At night, wild boars, deer, tapirs and many other animals make their way to the river. Above, on the trees, hardly distinguishable from the branches, the giant snakes lie in wait to swoop on their victims and strangle them. Once they have stayed their hunger with a deer or a wild boar, they drag themselves to the river bank and for weeks lie inertly in the warm waters to sleep their digestive sleep. At that time anyone can kill these monsters single-handed and I once destroyed one measuring forty-two feet.

Jaguars prowl and poisonous snakes use the night to wait along the beaches in the hope of catching turtles as they lay their eggs. Large fish dart into shallows in pursuit of huge schools of small fish who, in their panic to escape, will leap out of the water. During the night, we sometimes even heard the crunching and grinding of an alligator's jaw as it crushed a victim.

A little more than a month after our departure from Pucallpa we reached the capital of the province, the village of Requena. The newly appointed mayor was born in Germany, but had lived for over fifty years in this district. We arrived just as he was about to perform his first official function: the marriage of a native couple. The news of our arrival had reached the village ahead of us and instead of attending to the bride and groom he stood dressed in faultless white, waiting to receive us. His first act of official welcome was to invite us to his hut where we emptied a bottle of sugar-cane schnapps. When he remembered the bridal pair, the secretary who knew the form of the ceremony was missing. At last he was found, somewhat tipsy, in a village bar and the wedding ceremony began. The secretary mumbled undistinguishable words through an alcoholic mist and the mayor, standing close by, nodded regularly in approval. Then everybody stood round a thick leather-bound book to enter and sign their names. Since neither bride nor groom could write it was agreed to enter their real names at some later date.

Requena is a village with a special significance. Apart from lying on the Ucayali it also lies on the bank of the Rio Blanco, which combines with the Rio Tapiche just before it flows, at Requena, into the Rio Ucayali. Near the borders of Brazil and Peru, at the source of the Rio Blanco, live the Mayo Indians who, even today, are dangerous people, and Requena has been overrun by them many times the mayor told us. Not so very long ago they attacked the Catholic Mission of Requena and carried off two nuns and a monk. The Mayos who are notorious for abducting women probably thought the monk in his long habit was also a woman.

The naked and decapitated body of the monk was found in the jungle, but, although the Peruvian Government sent a punitive expedition to the district of the Mayos and bombed their settlements, the nuns were never traced. The Mayor believed that after taking their captives into the jungle, the mayos forced them to undress so that they would be naked like themselves; when they discovered the sex of the monk, they killed him in their disappointment and carried off the nuns as wives.

While we were emptying another few bottles with the mayor he introduced us to a twenty-three-year-old half-caste. His name was Missaels and ten years before he had been captured by the Mayos. His attackers tore off his clothes and rubbed his body with a foul-smelling root juice called Yerba. Missael's father and mother who lived on a farm on the Rio Blanco fired at the Indians who ran away leaving the boy behind them. Missael's mother immediately tried to wash off the stinking juice, but with little success, and the boy was almost driven crazy by the fearful smell of the ointment. During the month that followed the boy's only desire was to run away into the jungle after the Mayo Indians. The idea took hold of him like a disease and haunted him even in his dreams. His parents locked him up and guarded him, night and day, washing him every few hours in an attempt to dispel the maddening smell. It took a full three months before the boy was normal again.

When the Mayos need new hunting dogs they entice them to their camps with tasty meats and then rub them with these foul smelling roots. The dogs instantly forget their old masters and follow their new ones.

Two years ago an expedition of white men managed to reach the Mayos. Unnoticed by the explorers the Mayos had been shadowing them, but they did not harm the white men, probably fearing another punitive expedition. But the Campas Indians, who acted as the expedition's guides, were all murdered so that they could not bring other strangers to the land of the Mayos.

After two days we left Requena and the mayor, who had entertained us so generously with his stories and his schnapps. From here it was not very far to the geographic beginning of the Amazon and we reached this point in two hundred and eight drifting hours from Pucallpa. Here two large rivers—the Marañon and the Ucayali—combine into the immense river Amazon. People still argue which of them is its real source.

5

The Forbidden Zone

WE left our raft with Don Pedro, a half-caste planter, and told him we were going to visit the district of the Jivaros—the head-hunters of Ecuador.

I had been to this district in 1935, but had then approached it from the opposite direction, by way of the Andes; at that time I had spent some fascinating months with the Jivaros. I had become especially attached to a headman with whom I stayed and now I thought it would be nice to introduce my wife and daughter to this chieftain. I remembered the dozen or so shrunken heads hanging from the rafters of his hut and the threats of bitter vengeance from his enemies and wondered if he was still alive. He had never dared to leave the village without his body-guard and was not expected to survive much longer.

We were soon moving up the Rio Marañon in our motor-boat. We passed Concordia, Parinari and Nauta, and after eleven days reached the mouth of the Rio Pastaza. From here it was another few days to the mouth of the Rio Morona. We allowed ourselves two days' rest in Puerto America and then left to sail up the Rio Morona carrying a hundred and thirty gallons of petrol in three barrels and provisions for two months. After a week of smooth going we reached the first real rapids. We were now at the foothills of the Andes and were close to the borders of Ecuador. This was only a theoretical border without even a frontier patrol and we could not tell if we were still in Peru or already in Ecuador. The few Indians we met were friendly and astonished to meet white people, since apart from a few traders who sometimes visited the Indians to exchange manufactured rubbish for gold, this district was hardly ever visited.

Soon we forgot to count the days and our nerves became tense and brittle from the never-ending obstacles of rapids and racing currents. One or two of the Indians we met spoke a little Spanish and we learned that they called the river Morona the *Macuma,* which confirmed that we had crossed into Ecuador. The maps we had with us had long ceased to make any sense, and I began to doubt if we would ever find that tribe I had visited seventeen years before.

After passing no one for ages, we came quite suddenly upon the settlement of a largish tribe of half-civilised Indians. They told us it was madness to visit the Jivaros and that our undertaking would certainly end in tragedy. The Jivaros, they said, were the most savage of all men whose only abilities lay in the art of reducing human heads to the size of an orange without spoiling the accurate likeness. 'Don't go, your lives are in danger. No one has ever come back alive,' were their final words.

We thanked the Indians for their well-meant advice and left in the direction of the head-hunters, armed only with an old mouth-organ. I believed that as we were coming to them as a family on a friendly visit and without desire to change their way of life, the Jivaros would not harm us. I had faith that once the initial distrust was overcome we would be treated with the same respect we gave to them.

We had left our motor-boat with the Indians since we were by now very short of petrol and in any case it was doubtful if the small river which led to the Jivaros would have been navigable. In its place we had borrowed a dugout and paddled up river until our hands were raw. After four days we reached a little island with two crossed spears stuck firmly in the sand. This, we had been told in the village, was the sign of the head-hunters and a warning that we were entering forbidden territory.

Once past the island, thick jungle and deep loneliness surrounded us. We could think of nothing but the head-hunters and our first meeting with them. We had the uncomfortable feeling of being watched. Swiftly, without warning, night descended and we only just had time to find a camping site on a sandbank. Sitting by the flickering light of the fire in the black jungle night, I tried to keep my excitement and fear within manageable bounds. But I could not help worrying about our complete inability to defend ourselves should we be attacked and I tortured my conscience for having exposed my wife and daughter to this danger. Then I remembered my mouth-organ, a never failing friend in need, and soon the notes of the Tosselli 'Serenade' filled the jungle. This soothed my nerves but I still wondered how it would all end. Sleep, I thought, would be the only thing to bring me nearer to an answer.

As soon as dawn came I went to look for food and found delicious newly-laid turtle eggs; but I also found the fresh footprints of naked Indian feet in the wet sand. Had the Jivaros been near during the night? Had they watched us while we were asleep? Questions like this flooded my brain and received no answer. The next night I tried to soothe my nerves by playing Gounod's 'Ave Maria'. In the morning fresh footprints surrounded our camp. We felt naked, unprotected and frightened. During the third night we thought we recognised the sparkling eyes of Indians in the light of the flashing glow-worms.

On the fourth day we met the Jivaros and the unbearable tension was relieved. Wild and painted, with quick beats of their paddles and jabbering wildly amongst themselves in guttural voices, they approached the sandbank on which we were camping. There were six of them, four men and two women, in one dugout. We tried to look fearless and relaxed, and even Graciela, who must have felt the tense gravity of the situation, stood calmly watching the approach of the Indians. Before the dugout had touched the ground the Jivaros jumped out, gesticulating fiercely and talking in a high-pitched hysterical chatter.

The Indians started pushing and jabbing at me and trying to pull me by my arms into their boat. At first I fought back, but when they had torn almost all the clothes off my body I realised the hopelessness of our position and made them understand that we would go with them if they gave us time to gather up our belongings. Poor Graciela was terrified and clung to my wife's skirts and I, too, felt scared. Only Aenne seemed calm and col-

*Jivaro warrior
of the Rio Macumo*

*Shrunken head of white man,
the only one to come out of
the jungle, presented to the
author*

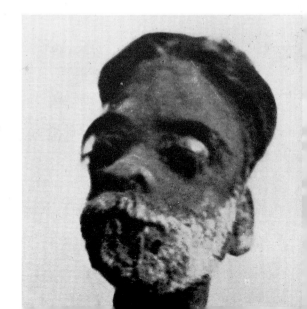

'*Tzanza*' *dance with shrunken head on spear*

Jivaro building a man-trap

lected, or perhaps she was so stunned at the suddenness of what we had been expecting for some time that she was unable to react. The sight of my calm wife reversed my reactions and I began to feel exhilarated by the idea of finding myself in the midst of such an infamous tribe. The great adventure had started in earnest.

At first the natives seemed to have some respect for my wife and child and only the women approached them. Soon, however, the eldest of them tried to stroke Graciela's golden hair, but Graciela kicked back like a wild horse. This amused the women and they responded with shrill laughter. Eventually Graciela and Aenne were dragged into the boat and we set off on our journey into the forbidden zone. Everybody paddled as hard as they could—even the women—since we were always moving upstream and the river was flowing fast. We travelled like this for about eight hours, without the natives taking much notice of us, until we reached a settlement of huts of wild sugar-cane leaves and bamboo standing round a clearing.

The Jivaros led us into a *choza*—a hut—that was uninhabited, and gestured to us that we could sleep there. After I had arranged our hammocks I decided to venture out to see if I could find something to eat, for we had had no food all day. Evening was approaching, it was very quiet and apart from a few toothless old women sitting in front of their huts chewing yuca fruits, no one was about. In front of one of the huts I recognised the old woman who had tried to stroke Graciela's hair. Behind her, hanging from a rafter, I could see a lovely bunch of golden ripe bananas.

It should not have been difficult to make her understand that I was hungry, but she misunderstood me all the same. She invited me to enter her hut and, once inside, the chase began. Perhaps she wanted a child from me, a white child with blue eyes and golden hair which she could stroke and play with! She began to pester me, driving me into a corner of the hut, where I clutched the bunch of bananas tightly in front of me wondering how I would ever be able to escape a fate said to be worse than death. The old woman now barricaded the door with a cross-

E

beam and with a lecherous smile on her toothless face came closer and closer. What was I to do? To offend her would probably have meant shrunken heads for the three of us. I decided that 'death rather than dishonour' was inappropriate to my particular situation. But when the old woman came so close that I was nauseated from the ghastly smell of the fermented masato on her breath, my fighting spirit was aroused.

I must have behaved exactly as we 'so-called' civilised people expect savages to behave. I jumped up, pushed the old woman away and showed her my claws by dancing wildly round her and screaming madly. My sudden violent outbrust gave her such a shock that she unbarred the hut and backed out in terror. I escaped to our hut—still clutching my bunch of bananas.

The next morning I was called to the *Curaca*—the chief of the tribe. As I walked through the village, flanked by two armed warriors, I had the feeling that I was being watched with enmity and suspicion. Had I offended the tribe last night by refusing the wishes of one of their elders? Or was I being summoned simply because we were strangers and intruders? The *Curaca* was an imposing elderly man, with a strong but not unkindly face and a pot belly. He looked at me cunningly and I had the horrible idea that he concentrated a long time on an inspection of my head. I felt most uncomfortable. There was no question of conversation since neither of us could understand the other. The *Curaca* talked at me for almost half an hour, gesticulating and getting more and more excited. I felt sure he was referring to the happenings of the previous evening. At last he paused long enough to realise that I had not understood what he was talking about and with an angry gesture he ordered me back to my hut.

For the next few days nothing happened. We were treated well and were allowed to move among the huts, but we were guarded night and day. It was obvious that we were not to be allowed to escape. It was uncanny, and unpleasant, to know there was something planned for us which we could do nothing about. Graciela was fascinated by her new surroundings and had made friends with some of the native children, but Aenne and I became tense and slept badly. I had dreams of being shut in a lion's cage, where I waited endlessly for the beast to pounce on me and tear me to bits. Aenne's dreams were very much like mine and it needed no subtlety to interpret our nightmares. We were happy when the mornings came and we could spend our time doing the household chores and walking about the settlement watching the natives.

The old women sitting in front of their simple sugar-cane and bamboo huts seemed to be almost entirely occupied with the chewing of the yuca fruit. They spat the cud into an earthenware pot and used it for the fermentation of masato. Masato is an alcoholic drink made of the yuca root and palm fruits. It is a foaming, rather thick, brown liquid, which has an acquired bitter-sweet taste and is not unlike beer. It does not taste too badly when one forgets how it is made. It is a very popular drink with almost all Indian tribes in large regions of South America. Vast quantities of it are consumed during festivities and the natives usually drink it until they are laid out in a stupor.

In our Jivaro camp each family had its own fireplace in front of the hut. The people eat very much the same sort of food that we had eaten during our journey. In addition to bananas which were eaten raw, boiled, fried or dried, the staple food was the yuca root which, like our potato, was eaten with fish, meat and vegetable dishes. One can eat this root freshly boiled, or peeled and dried and then grated and roasted over fire. This process produces a white or yellow powder, rougher in texture than ordinary flour. As there is a great variety of fish and animals in the jungle, and plenty of wild fruits, herbs, roots and vegetables, the diet of the Jivaros is much more varied than that of the ordinary people in the towns of South America.

Apart from cooking and looking after the babies, the women seemed to do most of the hard work. While they cut and fetched wood, collected food and carried water in heavy earthenware containers, the men were forever preparing for war, painting and decorating themselves and sharpening their weapons to avenge the blood feuds of past generations. They also hunted and caught fish and it was their responsibility, under the leadership of the medicine-men, to protect the tribe from evil demons. The men were the masters, the women slaves; the booty of war was always women, and a man would own as many as he could afford to feed. The best present a Jivaro man can give to someone he likes and respects is a new wife.

After one of the longest and most frightening weeks of my life, I was called to the *Curaca* again. The prospect that, at last, our fate was to be decided was a tremendous relief, although I feared that it might mean the end for the three of us. This time the *Curaca* and his ancient advisers were assisted by a young Indian who was able to speak a little Spanish. He had been especially summoned from afar to convey the chief's wishes to me. Now, at last I understood. The *Curaca*, the young Indian explained, wanted me to drive the evil demon from his sick son. If I succeeded I would win the friendship of the tribe and would be rewarded with anything I liked. If I did not succeed—the young Indian spared me the details, but I did not need any explanation.

The boy was brought to us and I noticed with relief and horror that he had a huge festering carbuncle on his head which gave him great pain. I learned from the Spanish-speaking Indian that various magicians had tried to cure the boy but the swelling had got worse. I could see at a glance that the pain had driven the poor youngster almost mad. What was I to do? Obviously a miracle was expected of me. I had once taken a first-aid course, but I felt terrified when I realised that I would now have to depend on this very limited knowledge to save the lives of Graciela, Aenne and myself.

I first of all questioned the boy and the chief, with the help of the Spanish-speaking Indian, about every detail in connection with this awful carbuncle. The boy, I learned, had injured himself while playing in the jungle. He had fallen into the undergrowth and a poisoned thorn had lodged in his skull. The thorn had been removed, but the wound had festered and would not heal. There was no doubt I would have to operate. My only instruments were a little vaccination knife, a small bottle of peroxide, an ordinary sewing needle with black thread, a magnifying glass which I used to light fires, a pair of tweezers and my razor.

'*Que dios me ayude*—so help me, God'—and I started the operation.

I began by clamping the boy's head securely between my legs. This caused excited exclamations from the tribe who had come to watch me and they surged frighteningly forward. Aenne, who knew that this was a matter of life and death, not only for the boy, but also for us, was near hysteria. So to calm and occupy her I asked her to hold back the onlookers. Then, holding the boy firmly, I soaped and washed his head. Despite his screams I drew my razor and removed the hair from around the wound. His cries grew more and more hysterical and the crowd again surged forward. This time my wife's terrified face and her desperate determination somehow instilled sufficient respect into the natives to allow me room to carry on.

The squeals of the boy subsided to a deep animal-like snorting and he struggled desperately to free himself. But my legs were as steel and he did not succeed in moving his head even a fraction of an inch from my grip. He must have suffered terrible pain by this manhandling and he fainted. The sudden silence that followed was startling. Before the boy or the onlookers could recover I drew my little knife and slashed open the growth. The pus spurted into my face and oozed thickly over his head. With the help of my magnifying glass I discovered that a tiny splinter of the poisoned thorn was still lodged in the skull. I pulled out the splinter with my tweezers and poured half-a-bottle of peroxide into the wound letting it foam until it was thoroughly clean. Then Aenne handed me the needle and thread which she had previously boiled and I sewed up the wound as best I could.

From the moment I had cut the carbuncle the natives had stood and gaped in breathless tension. When I had finished the sewing I asked the medicine-man, who had been watching with a critical professional eye, for some tobacco-leaves which he grudgingly gave me. I am sure he already saw my shrunken head hanging from the ceiling of his hut and did not want to be cheated of a prize trophy. I rolled a big cigar, lit it, and blew smoke over the body of the sick child to drive out the demons in Indian fashion. I had lit the cigar with my magnifying glass and this caused cries of astonishment from the natives. At last I dared to look up at my wife and daughter and their smiles of pride and love were something I shall cherish all my life.

As I was blowing smoke over the boy I suddenly realised that he was still unconscious and might die. Although I calmly continued to blow the smoke over him and massage him, my mind was in a wild panic. I had played my only card. Now there was nothing else I could do to save my family. It seemed to me that as life was fleeing from the boy, so it was also leaving me.

In a last desperate effort I searched my mind for a solution. Unexpectedly I remembered my boy scout days and the first-aid exercises for cases of drowning. Swiftly I began, pressed the used-up air out of the boy's lungs and, by moving his arms, pumped fresh air into them. This greatly impressed the natives who thought it a new magic. Then jubilantly I noticed the first faint signs of success. Slowly the boy began to breathe regularly again and a few minutes later he opened his eyes and looked at me with astonishment. I handed him to his father, who carried him carefully to his own hut and put him into his hammock. That evening the boy had already improved. His pains had lessened appreciably and my own head was fixed much more firmly on my shoulders.

From that time the Indians' attitude towards us changed and they no longer watched us with suspicion. However, their respect was mixed with fear because I had proved that I knew more than their own magician. His jealousy was so obvious that I was afraid he might persuade the tribe that I was in league with evil demons and should be killed. But the fact that the Indians believe firmly in life after death was in my favour. If I were killed, my ghost might continue to live in the same place as theirs and horrible retaliation would then be a certainty. Nevertheless, in the grip af alcohol or religious frenzy, anything could be expected of these wild and superstitious people.

The only person to whom I could cling was the Spanish-speaking Indian, Juan. As a child, Juan had been abducted by one of the last child-hunting bands that in the twenties combed the Amazon region. This band, led by fierce men, attacked one native village after another, massacring adults and carrying off the children. They tramped in a bedraggled caravan through the thickest jungle, and as fast as the children died from exhaustion, new ones were captured. When the caravan reached its destination forty children had survived, including Juan who had kept alert during the march and had remembered the rivers, mountain ranges and tracks which they had followed.

Juan was sold to a Spanish family in a mountain village where he had to work hard but was well treated. During the eight years he spent with the family he learnt Spanish. But the climate high up in the mountains was too raw for Juan and he ran away. He still vaguely remembered the way he had come and wandered down the hill until he reached a large river. Here he worked for some time in a saw-mill and for the first time in his life was paid in real money. As soon as he had saved a few coins he bought a little canoe. He drifted down the river and then paddled up one of its tributaries until he heard his mother tongue spoken. After some months of roaming he met our chief and because of the many useful things he had learned during his life in civilisation, he was treated with favour and respect. In any difficult situation Juan was always asked for his opinion and help.

Graciela had chosen the chief's son as her favourite playmate. In spite of the language difficulties the two understood each other very well. Her greatest achievement was to teach Tcha the game of hop-scotch. Indian boys do not usually play with girls, but as the little white girl was something special, Tcha condescended to play with her. Graciela taught everyone to play marbles and the glittering and mysterious-looking glass balls that she had brought into the wilderness were mixed with little round stones which she found on the river bank.

I think Tcha had fallen in love with Graciela for he followed her everywhere, brought her fruits and protected her from the dangers of the jungle. There was no question of any of the other boys teasing her or becoming too friendly with her. Tcha was never far from her side, serious and dignified, remaining always the chief's son. One day Graciela came running to me holding something in her hand and calling, 'Look, Papa, Tcha has given me this lovely present.' She was holding the shrunken head of a child in her hand. I was surprised as I had never heard of head-hunters shrinking children's heads and it must have been an especially valuable present. I never discovered in what circumstances this child's head had been shrunk. We all prefer not to know.

Weeks went by and we learned to make ourselves understood by sign language and a few words. Through playing with the Indian children all day long Graciela learned fastest and often when Juan was not with us she acted as our interpreter. We gradually took part in the natives' events and they began to accept us. Women came to our hut to show Aenne their babies or bring her an especially rare fruit; I was asked to accompany the men fishing or hunting and we were allowed to wander about freely.

It puzzled us for some time to see so many empty huts in the settlement, until we realised that whenever a death occurred the bereaved family moved out and built a new hut. This was done because they feared the ghosts of the dead.

The first thing every newly-married couple did after their wedding was to build a new home. This took about a day and relatives and friends would come to watch and give good advice. There was always a good deal of laughter and horse-play and some jocular friends would loosen the main bamboo strut so that the structure would often collapse just when the happy couple were ready to move in. Little fuss is made about marriage. The girls marry immediately after their first menstruation and the boys between sixteen and seventeen years of age. Once the first marriage has taken place, any further marriages depend entirely upon the wealth of the man concerned. There was a good deal of free and uncomplicated love-making among the tribe, especially after celebrations. During certain festivities the Jivaro women offered a pitcher of masato to a man, and if he wanted to make love to her he would have to empty the pitcher in one gulp. If he was too drunk, or too old, to empty it, the woman would take it from him and empty the remains over his head, much to the hilarious amusement of the bystanders.

Having babies was as uncomplicated as making love. Aenne watched the birth of several Jivaro babies because the women seemed to think her presence would drive away bad spirits. When a Jivaro baby is about to be born, the woman calls her husband and they go to a tree with a firm branch within easy reach. She grips the branch and pulls herself up by her arms and while she is actually hanging the baby is born. The Jivaro man catches the baby, severs the cord with his teeth and then the couple bathe the newly born baby in a nearby brook and give it its first feed. After only a short rest the mother goes back to work while the proud father relaxes with the new baby in his hammock.

There is no doubt that the Jivaro men have a good life. The more women the tribe possesses, the more prosperous is the tribe. So they supplement their supply by going on expeditions to kidnap women from others. The medicine-man, the spiritual leader, decides on a suitable time for the expedition, but if he makes a mistake in his timing he is likely to lose his head, which is hung from a tree as a warning to future practitioners.

The only thing the Jivaros plant are coca-leaves and these, too, are tended by the women. The ripe leaves are dried and, with the addition of other herbs, are ground into a dry powder. They take the powder by blowing it into each other's nostrils. This seemed to us a much better way of taking the drug than the continuous chewing practised by the Indians of Peru.

It was amazing how much brewing, grating, straining and mixing was always going on near the medicine-man's hut. He was usually surrounded by a battery of highly-decorated pots as he prepared magic brews or medicines. He was too jealous to allow us to watch him closely, suspecting us of wanting to steal his magic formulae, or fearing we would cast an evil spell on his preparations. Some of his brews seemed to be surprisingly effective, and I really believe that the Jivaros can heal leprosy. While we were there one of the tribe was attacked by this ghastly disease and his ear had become horribly deformed. I watched the medicine-man putting strange leaves soaked in plant juices on his ears, and after a few days of this treatment the wound began to heal.

Poisons had a special fascination for the tribe and their effectiveness enhanced the standing of the *Brujo*—the magician—more than anything else. As far as we could find out, the curare was the basis of the many different poisons in use. After a new lot of poison had been prepared by the *Brujo* we watched it being tested. Some of it, mixed with seeds, was given to a tame parrot, which collapsed after the first few pecks. Had it not worked efficiently, the medicine-man would have been blamed for allowing an evil spirit to interfere and weaken the poison. This curare poison is not only used against the enemy when head-hunting, but also for the hunting of edible animals. Curare is only muscle paralysing, but if administered in sufficient quantities will paralyse the heart and lungs and cause death. The meat of the animal killed with this poison can be safely eaten.

The Jivaros use poisons such as sanango, barbasco and ayaguaca for fishing. In this case they dissolve the roots which contain the poisons in a dugout filled with water. Then the dugout is towed to a place where a little river forms a small lake and the substance is tipped into the water. The fish draw the poison through their gills and are immediately paralysed and float to the surface.

The Indians would take me on their hunting expeditions, but they never offered me the use of their spears or blowpipes. I was only allowed to watch for Jivaros do not share their hunting secrets with strangers and always had a personal guard close by me. This was to protect me, since I was unarmed, and to stop me from running away or using evil magic. One day when we went hunting they left me in the jungle far from the village, guarded only by an armed boy of about fifteen. When night fell and the huntsmen had not returned, I took the opportunity to run away and make my own way home. I wandered round all night and got back when the sun was almost at its zenith. The Indians did nothing to me, but at dawn they had returned to the place where they had left me and given the poor boy a good hiding for not having guarded me properly.

When we had been living for several months with the Jivaros, we thought it was time to return. All our belongings and our raft were back at the starting point of our adventure, with Pedro the planter, and he might easily imagine that we had been eaten, shrunk, or made into slaves by the head-hunters. It worried me to think that he might have disposed of our raft and all our household belongings.

One day I noticed that the *Brujo* was looking at me with particular malice as he walked pompously to the hut of the chief, resplendent in his painted decoration. One by one a great number of Jivaro men entered the chief's hut and we could hear an ever-increasing monotonous and yet exciting humming from the inside of the hut. This humming continued for almost two days and nights and there was little doubt that something was in preparation. The women sat in front of their huts busily chewing and spitting the yuca juice into their small earthenware bowls, while the men gathered in little groups sharpening their hardwood spears. Outside the medicine-man's hut stood a large quiver full of freshly poisoned arrows.

During the evening of the third day the drums began to roll and a large bonfire was lit in front of the chief's hut. The entire tribe and guests from neighbouring tribes, Graciela, Aenne and I assembled. The entrance to the *Brujo*'s hut was closed with a palm-leaf curtain. When it was ceremoniously opened by the chief's son, the chief stepped out in full war regalia, followed by the *Brujo*, looking very fierce, and seven Jivaro men. They were staring absently into space as if in a concentrated trance and I suspected that they were in a narcotic dream. All of them wore magnificent headgear of coloured feathers, with colours of red, yellow and blue predominating. Round their necks were strings of dried jungle fruits of many shades, and their bodies were painted with exotic designs.

The seven warriors, armed with spears and blowpipes, danced slowly round the fire swinging their spears, while the *Brujo*, murmuring magic formulae, threw handfuls of powder into the fire which flashed whitish-blue flame. He then took several pieces of wood and traced circles and signs over the flames before he threw them into the fire. This ritual was to prevent hostile demons from interfering with the plans for the night. Quite suddenly the seven warriors vanished into the jungle. Aenne and I began to suspect that we had just witnessed the beginning of a head-hunting expedition. Would we be allowed to see the end as well, we wondered?

The head-hunt is an ancient ritual among the tribes, a kind of vendetta reaching back for endless generations. Almost the only heads sought are those of enemy head-hunters. The family of a beheaded Jivaro is bound by honour to capture the head of the slayer, so that the victim's spirit may be admitted to the land of the ghosts, the heaven of the Jivaros.

When the warriors had gone, a series of dances started in honour of the ghosts protecting them. I was drawn into the midst of the dancers while Aenne and Graciela watched me with apprehension and surprise from a distance. Even Graciela, who wanted to do everything, was silenced by her father's strange behaviour. But I was oblivious to all this. I let my limbs follow the throbbing beat of the drums and forgot that I was different from the naked, sweating figures pounding the dust. The masato I had drunk had tasted disgusting, but it fired my blood and drove me to a frenzy so that I simply had to continue dancing and drinking and drinking and dancing until I collapsed in exhaustion. I awoke when dawn was breaking to find myself lying in the dust amongst the dark bodies of the natives. I made my way home to our hut and collapsed again in my hammock.

When I awoke the second time the warriors had just returned. From the radiant face of the *Brujo* and the fact that, for once, he did not pierce me with his hate-filled eyes, I knew that the hunt had been successful. I watched from some bushes a little distance off as the *Brujo* chose the warriors who would have the great honour of assisting him in the head-shrinking ceremony. Then he turned, walked slowly to his hut, and vanished inside. There was complete silence until he reappeared carrying an Indian head before him and, after a few measured steps, carefully placed it on a small mat on the ground. Its black hair was neatly brushed in a straight fringe over the forehead, the eyes wide and staring, the mouth half-open and the cheek-bones exaggeratedly protruding. With its even grey-brown colour set off against the black hair and blood ringed neck, the head looked like a horribly realistic stage prop for Macbeth.

The *Brujo* chewed a few tobacco-leaves and allowed the juice to drip into the nostrils of his assistants to make them immune to hostile magic. The chosen six lined up and, one after another, dipped the point of their lances into the blood dripping from the throat of the recently-severed head. Then the medicine-man took a sharp hardwood knife and with lightning speed made some cuts in the skin at the back of the head. Now he could pull the skin apart, and in one smooth action he pulled the scalp from back to front, turning it inside out, like skinning a rabbit. By making small cuts at the mouth, nose and eyes he was able to loosen the facial skin without damaging it. He completed the operation by pulling off the entire skin of the head in one piece. The cuts were sewn up with a bamboo needle and fine fibres, and only the opening at the neck remained. The lips were also sewn up so that the victim's curses would not harm the tribe.

In the meantime fires had been lit and a large pot placed in the middle of one of them. This earthenware pot was specially designed and had been carefully decorated and fired. After the pot had been filled with cold river water, the skin of the head, now freed of all bones, was dropped into it. To stop the hair falling out, the skin was removed the moment the water started boiling. Only a head with hair is acceptable as a trophy.

More fuel was put on the fire and the sand underneath brought to an intense heat. Some of the hot sand was then poured through the opening of the throat by the medicine-man. This treatment continued every two hours for two days and nights. As soon as the head was filled with hot sand it was ironed and pressed with hot stones wrapped in palm-leaves. After forty-eight hours the magic had worked. The head of the hateful enemy was shrunk to the size of a fist. The thing looked like an old mop with long hair hanging over a tiny wrinkled face now tanned tough as leather. Finally, to preserve the trophy indefinitely, the head was smoked over a fire prepared with a special green wood which gave off clouds of thick smoke.

Now the victory feast could begin. The warriors who had

taken part in the head-shrinking ceremony lined up with their blood-covered red spears in front of them. The man who had done the killing perched the shrunken head on his lance and slowly the group began to move in a dance, their naked feet thumping the ground in low rhythmical thuds in time with the guttural sing-song of the rest of the tribe. Another great victory over the hated enemy had been won, with the head as proof of the heroic deed. And so vengeance will continue—a head for a head—without end.

After the feast everybody lay about sick from overeating and drinking, and we decided to take advantage of the general apathy to get away. Before anybody had realised what had happened Graciela, Aenne, Juan and I had jumped into a dugout and raced down the whirling stream. Juan had become my friend and he took us to the place where the two crossed spears stood on the little island. I promised that I would return, and explained that I was only leaving for a short time to see if all was well with my own tribe.

Night came again, but this time we were not afraid. Thousands of glow-worms flew around us, but they did not make us see threatening eyes spying from the dark. After a swift journey downstream we arrived at our starting point, to the great amazement of Pedro and the half-civilised Indians who had already imagined us as shrunken heads on the spears of the head-hunters. Ten nights after we had left we were again sleeping in the luxury and comfort of our cosy balsa raft, tied up to Don Pedro's jetty. We had been away for barely four months and yet it felt as if we had returned home from some fantastic weird fairy-tale existence. We still have Graciela's prize possession, the shrunken head of a child, to prove to ourselves that we had not been dreaming.

6

The Amazon

AFTER the excitement of staying with the Jivaros we could think of nothing more pleasant than drifting down the Amazon. For days after we left Don Pedro's nothing happened to disturb the timeless paradise of the luscious, steaming jungle. But no paradise on earth will last for ever and after a week ours came to an end. Flashes of lightning announced the arrival of violent thunderstorms.

The river was very wide now, and as we had learned that the storms usually came upstream, and from the right, we took advantage of the protection that the wooded banks on this side of the river afforded us. Whoever detected the first signs of an approaching storm—a gust of wind, a drop of rain or a cloud on the horizon—would call 'action stations' and I would jump into the motor-boat, start the engine and steer for the bank. Aenne would prepare the ropes and Graciela would see to it that everything on deck was securely fastened. Then we would tie the raft to one of the giant trees until the storm was over. After little more than ten minutes the thunderstorm, which lashed up waves big enough to terrify the most experienced sailor, vanished.

The nights, during which we often continued to drift downstream by the light of the moon, lost their peace and perfection and patches of fog would quite suddenly restrict visibility. There was now a certain amount of shipping on the river and fruit laden rafts drifted past us in the middle of the stream, using their big oars to make the best use of the fast-running water. The crews knew the river inside out and gained at least four

69

hours in twelve on us, but we thought it safer to stay in the slow current near the bank.

One morning a thick fog enveloped us so that we could not see from one end of the raft to the other and soon lost all sense of direction and movement as we were not only drifting downstream but also turning round on our axis. We constructed a fog-horn out of a frying-pan and kitchen utensils and Graciela thought it wonderful fun to be allowed to make as much noise as she liked all day. Aenne and I were far less amused. Frustration and fear overcame us as we floated through the endless haze. Made desperately tired by staring into the shapeless grey, we both nodded off, until we woke with a start imagining a huge obstacle looming up in front of our tired eyes. But there was only silence until a strange thumping noise caught our attention. It was moving towards us steadily and after about ten minutes we knew that a steamer was heading our way.

Slowly the sound became louder and louder. We felt utterly helpless and had no idea where we were or where we could find the protecting bank of the river. We almost panicked and were tempted to jump overboard rather than wait for the crash. Making as much noise as she could on our kitchen utensils, Graciela, at least, was happy so in desperation we joined in. In a moment a giant black cloud came rushing towards us, and before we had time to panic our raft had bumped the hull of a ship. It was a gun-boat and fortunately it stopped at the sound of our tin-pot orchestra. An officer climbed down to investigate us, but soon departed with a somewhat sarcastic farewell.

Shortly after that incident the fog lifted and we drifted under a blue sky. From a *Balsa de Carga*—a freight balsa—which we overtook I learned that we were about six hours' drifting time from Iquitos. In an effort to reach Iquitos before darkness I towed the raft with the motor-boat but we did not gain much time.

Night came and we could see no sign of the town. At last at eleven o'clock hundreds of cheerfully twinkling lights greeted us, but we could not find the entrance to the harbour. The town is situated on a small river running into the Amazon and we had

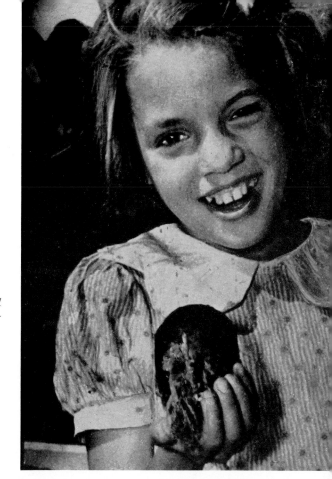

Shrunken head of a child presented to Graciela by the chief's son (see page 62)

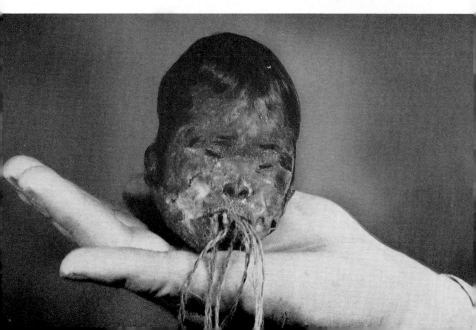

The balsa-rafts' harbour at Iquitos

Tucuna Indian girl

Graciela with Anaconda

to be careful not to drift past it. We had also been warned not to get into the current of the river which might crush us against the town jetty. I was so confused by the complicated instructions that various well-wishers had given me, that I was over-cautious and navigated too close to land and kept sticking on mudbanks. It was daylight before we reached the harbour.

The first thing I had to do was to replenish our empty cash-box and, with this purpose in mind I arranged an exhibition of the photographs I had taken on the trip. The cathedral authorities lent me the church hall and as the people went to Mass regularly my exhibition was well-attended. Everybody willingly paid a small entrance fee to be allowed to look at the pictures of their wild brethren.

A few days later we tied up below the town next to a five-thousand-ton Norwegian steamer. Kon-Tiki was still fresh in everybody's mind and the Norwegians showed a lively interest in our raft. The crew had heard that we had come from the land of the head-hunters and had been given some shrunken heads, so we had lots of visitors. Each visitor brought a present with him—a bottle of beer or a bottle of their lovely aquavit—and Graciela collected half-a-suitcase of sweets.

To the good and pious people of Iquitos the Norwegian seamen seemed like heathens or the reincarnation of the devil. During a Sunday outdoor concert when the girls were promenading around the plaza, some of the sailors took a bath in the cool waters of the fountain, wearing only their underwear. Others dressed up as Indians from the interior with brightly coloured headgear and painted torsos and ambushed some of the citizens on their way home from church. After the confusion and panic had subsided and the local inhabitants had realised that the whole thing was a joke, they discovered that many of their daughters had vanished with the retreating attackers. Angry fathers and distressed mothers stormed the police station. Next morning the captain of the ship had to ransom his sailors from the gaol.

After sixteen days in Iquitos we decided to continue our journey but before we left the business community of the town

F

gave us a most useful store of tinned provisions. Our departure was not exactly glorious, but no doubt it was entertaining to the crowd of onlookers who saw us off. As I was towing the raft into the middle of the river the motor failed and we collided with a Peruvian gunboat. The sailors on board cheered us wildly and when finally the engine started and I slowly got the raft away, they whistled and called after us. One wag shouted that our boat had only eight chicken-power.

Next evening we reached the settlement of Indiana which was looked after by Canadian Catholic missionaries. The day was Sunday and Graciela and Aenne went to Mass. The Indian canoes, heavily laden with families, arrived from distant parts. I had asked the priest to try and find some Indians to help wedge two new balsa trunks under the raft as the old trunks were so full of water by now that the floor of our hut was almost submerged. I arrived at the little wooden church just before the end of the service and heard the priest appeal for helpers. Quite a number of Indians volunteered to assist me.

The repairs took some time and caused a lot of merriment. To get the first new long trunk under the water we had to sit on it like birds on a telegraph wire. The trunk kept turning and we were constantly thrown into the water. In the end we succeeded in cajoling it into position and this lifted the raft three inches. With a bump the second trunk slipped into position and the raft rose above water-level.

Three days after our departure from Indiana we reached the mouth of the powerful Rio Napo, which has its source in Ecuador, near Quito. This is the place where the Amazon, the greatest river in the world, officially begins.

Four hundred years ago a Spanish explorer called Francisco Orellana discovered this region and reported to his Government that he had found an Indian tribe consisting entirely of warrior women. He christened them, appropriately, 'The Amazons' and the river, on the banks of which these women lived, 'Rio Amazonas'.

These Amazons, it was said, enticed men from neighbouring tribes to wild celebrations and orgies, but when the feasting was over the men had to depart in a hurry or be murdered. Every male child born as a result of these orgies was killed at birth by the Amazons.

The Rio Napo had a different rainy season from the Amazon and we ran into heavy rain clouds, and the downpours created giant whirlpools. We were caught in one of them, and in spite of all my efforts we turned round and round for hours on end. Again luck came to our rescue, this time in the shape of a huge flood wave which came swelling from the Napo into the Amazon and catapulted us out of the whirlpool.

Three days later we reached Pebas, a town close to the border of Peru, Brazil and Colombia. Pebas is an important strategic point; towering about three hundred feet above the river its guns can prevent any ship from passing. Garrison duty at these lonely frontier posts is not popular and in some cases its officers and men have been posted there for particular or disciplinary reasons.

We drifted on, and after another three days stopped at the mouth of the Rio Mayoruna. On the river bank was a beautiful plantation owned by a Peruvian who invited us to stay with him. Two Yagua Indians had just arrived, each carrying a heavy load of rubber which they wished to exchange for knick-knacks, salt, nails and other useful commodities. These two were well known to our host and with his help we persuaded them to take us to their settlement a few days' march away.

The Yaguas live by a small river called the Ampiyacu. From time to time they visit the civilised regions with their families and work in the fields of the planters. As soon as they have received their payment which is always made in kind, they return to their homes in the jungle.

We left at sunrise for the Yaguas camp but our guides went too fast for Aenne, Graciela and myself. The two Indians moved along the jungle paths in a sort of jog-trot, despite the heavy baskets they carried, and the leader had to stop and wait for us every few minutes. With only my old shot gun to carry I could not keep up, and Graciela and Aenne were soon exhausted.

The jungle was damp and mouldy and in spite of the deep

shade the sweat poured from our bodies. Huge water-drenched spiders' webs, glittering like diamonds, barred our way and clung to our faces. We had to cross many rivers on slippery tree-trunks on which the Indians balanced like graceful tight-rope walkers, but over which we slid clumsily on our stomachs. It was not difficult to guess what the two natives thought of us, but they were patient. The leader carried Graciela most of the way while the other took my shotgun and Aenne's bundle.

We stayed the night in a *tambo*, a local inn—a simple palm-leaf and bamboo hut which the natives can erect within minutes. It is little more than a hut without walls and close under the roof is an attic covered with thin branches to sleep on, or to store things in a dry and safe place. We soon had a cheerful fire going on the clay floor and the blue, pleasant-smelling smoke gave us a feeling of home and complete contentment. The two Indians disappeared into the brush to shoot a bird or monkey and in the distance we could hear the cries of animals. Aenne and Graciela squatted by the fire, and an aroma of freshly-brewed coffee filled the air.

I went to look for dry wood and met our two guides who had just killed a monkey with a poisoned arrow. When they had skinned and cleaned the animal in a nearby brook, it looked so much like a human being that I was sure Aenne and Graciela would refuse to eat it. I asked the Indians to hack it to pieces and throw the head, feet and tail away and told Aenne that we had a shot a hare. The meat tasted delicious. There are many people in the jungle, including Europeans, who live entirely on monkey meat.

When night fell and Graciela was fast asleep, my wife and I relaxed in our hammocks, smoking and listening to the sounds from the darkness. The whole jungle seemed to be alive with chirping, quacking, squealing, growling and crying. The noise crackled in the bushes and whispered in the tree-tips. Behind our mosquito nets we felt safe and relaxed and idly following the glow-worms drawing strange patterns in the darkness we dropped off to sleep.

After a further two days' march we reached the Yagua village. At first the Indians were reserved, but suspicion soon gave way to curiosity and when we handed out small presents of fish-hooks, mirrors, matches, salt and tobacco we became popular. The Yaguas tended small plantations of yuca, maize and pepper fruits. They used long blowpipes with poisoned arrows to shoot birds and made ornaments in wonderful and varied colour combinations and designs from tiny bird's feathers. The Yaguas were probably the most artistic of the tribes we met during our journey, and the small containers and ornaments they made from thousands and thousands of feathers were gay and original in design. This freshness and good taste was also reflected in the dress of the women. They wore charming little skirts made of thin plant fibres and a headgear like a crown made of countless multi-coloured bird feathers. They also wore a delicately shaped feather ornament on their breasts and featherbands round their arms and knees.

The Yagua women were sweet to Aenne and gave her a skirt and the ornaments belonging to it. As long as the native men and women were sober they were always exceedingly polite to my wife and never talked to her roughly. In general the women were much more reserved than the men and would show their emotion openly only in their love of their children. I have never seen an Indian woman show signs of affection towards a man unless they were a little drunk, and then only on rare occasions.

In spite of the fact that girls become mothers from the age of ten onwards, the Yaguas have an unusually happy family life. Unfortunately many babies die from worms, or from the results of drinking polluted water. I tried to make them realise that drinking water should be boiled, but they could not understand. They believed that disease comes from demons who planted evil seed in the helpless bodies of their babies.

The Yaguas are well known as boat builders. They hollow out huge trees and shape them into beautiful dugouts. When the rains flood the Amazon for hundreds of miles, they take their canoes to the big river to sell them. In the dry season the jungle in the region is full of game, monkeys, jaguars, huge nutria, deer, hares and giant anaconda snakes. The flood waters of the Amazon leave huge fish such as sea-cows, large pike, fish otters and a multitude of others in the lakes and marshes. The Yagua men spend much of their time collecting wild rubber, slashing the trees and collecting the milk in little cups. In the evenings this liquid is poured over a slowly-turning stick above a fire until it thickens. A growing rubber ball is formed this way and when it weighs about eighty pounds the Yaguas carry it to the nearest trader.

We took many photographs in the village once I had convinced the Indians that we had no evil intentions. I showed them photographs of tribal brothers who lived near Pebas. They even knew one of them and kept passing the photograph round screaming with laughter. In the end everybody wanted to be photographed. Usually, Indians are very camera-shy and often a photographer takes his pictures in mortal danger. Haste can have fatal consequences. The rule is to let the natives get used to you first and then wait patiently for a suitable moment. Not long ago a visiting American flashed his camera at some natives suddenly appearing from a thicket, and within seconds he had collapsed under a hail of poisoned arrows.

At first every Indian sees a camera as a weapon which threatens his life, or at least one that will bring him bad luck. He attacks in self-defence. Quite a few natives familiar with photography believe that a picture of themselves robs them of their soul.

We left the Yaguas on good terms and returned to our raft. As we were drifting happily downstream once more, we saw a speedboat racing towards us. The six people in it wore long, white, flowing coats and their heads were covered in white. They looked like doctors ready for the operating theatre. Doctors, in fact, they were. They boarded our raft and told us not to tie up on the right bank of the river as we were close to the leper colony of San Pablo. They took a great interest in us and invited us to visit the colony.

This leper settlement is an entirely self-sufficient community, with its own workshops, farm and fishery. Most of the five hundred and fifty lepers come from the poorer classes. Unfortunately the better-off lepers who had families to support them remained in the towns. The state is allowed to commit a leper to the settlement by force, but does so only in extreme cases. Often the healthy partner in a marriage is left behind and in that case a leper is allowed to contract a new marriage with another leper in the settlement. This marriage is even recognised by the Catholic church. The children from such unions are born healthy and drink the milk of the sick mother for two months. Two years later the children are separated from their parents and the state looks after them. The station is administered by the Catholic Church and run by Franciscan monks and Canadian sisters. The nurses and assistants are lepers trained by the doctors. Up to the time of our visit not one of the doctors or other healthy people in the settlement had caught the disease, although I noticed that none of the sisters appeared to be very careful.

The patients live in rather dilapidated wooden shacks. If they are fit, and wish to, they can get paid work in the plantations, workshops and fisheries. Not wanting to take risks with Graciela, we left the leper settlement the same afternoon. As we slowly drifted away the members of the colony stood on the banks waving, and we had the feeling that they followed the raft with longing as it drifted towards freedom.

Next morning we tied up on the right bank at the Peruvian Customs Station of Chimbot. Formalities were simple and on leaving we found that we had some gay and colourful stowaways on board; parakeets from the Amazon, playmates for Graciela. These parakeets looked like a cross between parrots and budgerigars, and could be taught to talk quite easily. Graciela soon made friends with our new companions and by evening they all had names. One was called 'Struwel Peter', because he had untidy plumage, another 'Yellow Head' and a third 'Noddy', because he nodded his head when he tried to speak. The fourth was called 'Cheeseeater' but her favourite was 'Mister'. He could say 'mister' so beautifully that we sometimes imagined there was another person on the raft.

We now had Colombian territory on the left bank and Peruvian territory on the right. That night we stayed at the mouth of a little river called Zancudo Parana, the river of the large stinging mosquito. It certainly lived up to its name. At sundown we were attacked by clouds of mosquitos, and, standing well protected behind our screen on the verandah, we watched a fantastic spectacle. All evening and half the night we did not dare go outside lest the swarms of mosquitos sucked the last drop of blood from our bodies. When a swarm settled on the netting it was so thick that we could not look through it. I put my hand against the netting to see what would happen and within seconds I was scorched by the poison from hundreds of tiny stings. My hand swelled into a painful lump. Countless ornamental fish of all shapes and sizes, however, feed on the mosquito brood, so they cannot all be so poisonous.

We met a man in Leticia who made a living collecting these little fish and sending them by chartered plane every two weeks to Florida. Graciela never tired of dipping her butterfly net into the water and bringing up different varieties of pretty little fish. She put them in containers and fed them regularly. So with the birds, her butterfly collection, her drawing book and the fish she was busy from morning till night.

Next morning we passed the narrowest part of the Amazon, just about three hundred feet wide. Here the raging torrent forces itself between two hills, and as there was no other way through we had to risk it. The waters were running so fast that I could not manoeuvre the heavy raft. I simply let it shoot down, closed my eyes and prayed. Strangely nothing happened to us and the stream, or fate, steered us with a sure hand past all obstacles.

The same day we landed at Leticia, a village which had only recently been ceded to Colombia after the war against Peru. It was a busy place, kept prosperous for prestige and strategic reasons. We decided that it might be a good thing to pay our respects to the commandant and on the way to see him we met an engineer in charge of the local airport which was being enlarged. He immediately offered me work as a tractor driver. I accepted at once. Colombian pesos have a high exchange value in Brazil and as we were soon going to be in that country it would not do us any harm to have a little cash in reserve.

My first vehicle was a large sandtip with the driving seat at the back. The wheels were larger than myself and the giant mechanical shovel loaded the truck so full that a mountain of sand obscured my sight entirely. It was very awkward, especially when I had to drive backwards up the steep loose bank of the river from where I got the sand. I was always afraid that the whole contraption would trundle head-over-heels into the river. I had never driven anything like a tractor before, but in South America one has to have enough confidence to tackle everything that comes along. To my surprise I quickly graduated into the most efficient driver on the Leticia airfield. After my first successful run I had a drink in one of the many drinking huts. The bartender told me that the engineer had had bad luck with his tractor drivers lately. The last one had driven over a child and was now imprisoned by the commandant. It was only after I had downed a second glass of schnapps that I suddenly remembered that the engineer made a special point of telling me that I must never let the engine of my sandtip stall. If I did, a giant tractor would have to be brought from the other side of the airfield to push it until it started. Of course, my motor had stopped in front of the liquor shack—and that was during the first few hours of my employment!

Day after day I deposited loads of sand on the shadeless airfield. We were on the Equator and the sun burned without pity; all metal parts became blistering hot and to prevent my hands from scorching I drove in thick leather gloves. I developed a most painful stiff neck through the continuous backwards driving, and was hardly able to get my head straight when work was done. When we had cloudbursts the airfield turned into a gigantic morass where one got hopelessly stuck. Within minutes the sun would beat down again and change it to a rock-hard, bumpy surface. Sometimes a jaguar crossed my path and, safe on my high driver's seat, I would chase the terrified animal back into the jungle.

One day while I was tipping a load of sand on the middle of the airfield the engineer came racing towards me in his car. The sky had darkened with a huge, thick thundercloud and the wind was beginning to rise. He skidded to a halt in front of me, dragged me into the car, and raced at breakneck speed to the harbour. On the way he explained that a twelve thousand ton passenger liner, a relic used as a troopship by the Colombians in the war with Peru, had broken its moorings and was about to squash my raft like a pancake. Aenne and Graciela were on board.

I was horrified and before the car stopped I was already out and sprinting to the raft. I found Aenne and Graciela calm and safe, surrounded by a crowd of onlookers. Graciela was carrying her birdcage with the five parakeets to safety and my wife had bundled together our most precious belongings and was ready to leave the raft across a gangplank. There was nothing for us to do but stand by and watch the destruction of our beloved home.

Slowly but surely, the giant hull loomed closer to our poor, minute raft. Not a sound came from the crowd. Graciela buried her head in my lap because she could not bear to watch what was about to happen and Aenne held my hand tightly. Now the inevitable was going to happen. I held my breath. A splintering and grinding crash and the protruding roof of our hut was torn to pieces. Then silence. Tension mounted as we awaited the final crash. But nothing happened. Slowly, like awakening from a nightmare, I realised that the liner had stopped. Thanks to the shallow bank it had grounded the moment it hit our overhanging roof.

It was a miracle and Aenne and I fell into each others arms. We had to calm Graciela who could not stop crying. The crowd of onlookers were jumping and dancing around us with pleasure, slapped us on the back and congratulated us on our good fortune.

I had been working on the airfield now for thirty days, thirty days of driving backwards, and my neck had become terribly stiff. I could not carry on and found a job pulling a heavy roller back and forth over the new airstrip. But the boredom was too much for me and I was longing to continue our journey. As I had earned enough money to buy some provisions and two fifty-gallon drums of petrol, I decided to retire.

When we drifted past Leticia many people stood on the shore and waved us goodbye. About lunchtime we reached Tabatinga, the Brazilian frontier town, where our passports had to be stamped again. Now we were in Brazil and so we had to change from talking Spanish to Portuguese. It was amazing how Graciela managed to make herself understood after only a few days. A few weeks later while Aenne and I were still struggling hard and getting mixed up with Spanish, she was speaking Portuguese fluently.

The plantations along the river became more numerous and when we discovered that the Brazilian farmers were growing vegetables we enjoyed a change of diet. Our food was entirely decided by geography. From Pucallpa to Iquitos we had oranges, guayna bananas, lemons, fried bananas, fish and rice and some chicken and duck. From Iquitos to Leticia it was nearly always rice and black beans. Now we had vegetables, cucumbers, water-melons, fried green bananas, rice and black beans and, of course, fish. We also had farinha and yuca which are eaten with every meal in this part of Brazil.

During the next day a heavy thunderstorm closed in on us. Within minutes the blue sky was a threatening black, and the rising storm had whipped up the calm waters. I decided to land and jumped into the motor-boat in order to drag the raft to the safety of the shore. But just before we got there I ran out of petrol. The thunder-cloud had nearly reached us and it was almost dark. The wind became increasingly strong, humming and rustling through the *palasadas*. I knew that within minutes the high waves would make the raft uncontrollable. There was no solution but to jump into the water and try to drag the raft with a rope, inch by inch, towards the shore. I did it with seconds to spare and managed to tie the rope to an overhanging tree. The rain came down in sheets and our raft was thrown about by the wild waves. The storm was still increasing when I noticed that the raft had started to drift upstream against the strong current past the *palasadas* that we had safely outman-oeuvred just before. The branches ripped deep gashes in the thin walls of the hut, but the rope held fast. I decided that we simply had to get away from the bank, so I jumped into the motor-boat, filled the tank with petrol, started the engine, cut the rope and dragged the raft out into the stormy river. We still drifted upstream, but at least we were out of reach of the dangerous *palasadas*.

As suddenly as it had come, the storm vanished, the sky was blue again and once more the river was as calm as a mirror. It was lovely and cool, and for once the sun felt pleasantly warming instead of uncomfortably hot. We floated peacefully through the jungle accompanied by pairs of ara birds (macaws) gliding in slow circles above us, while the screams of the ever-present howler monkeys followed us incessantly along the river banks.

A few days later we reached Santa Rita do Weil, a settlement dating from the rubber boom, and founded by German settlers around 1870. We had been told about a man named Geissler who was passionately fond of telling stories of the old pioneering days, and who once he found an audience, would keep it listening to him for weeks on end. I thought it would be interesting to meet him.

Geissler's house was hidden behind the river bank and the fast current carried us past his place. So we tied up near the home of another German called Baxmann, an ex-professor from Berlin. Geissler arrived a few minutes later. He had seen us drift by and had jumped into his little dugout to make sure we would not escape him.

7

Santa Rita do Weil

THE last of the original pioneers left in Santa Rita do Weil were our new friends Geissler and Baxmann, both of whom were in their seventieth year. In spite of the climate, which is supposed to be murderous, they had kept wonderfully fit and looked twenty years younger than they really were.

Henry Geissler, who had said he only wanted to have a look at the raft, stayed for three nights without going home, although his house was only half-an-hour away. He had so much information and was so enthusiastic about his adopted country that we hardly noticed that Henry went on talking day after day. We offered him a hammock, but he preferred to sleep on the hard deck of the raft. Before he lay down he stripped and dived into the Amazon. The large stinging mosquitos sat in thick layers on his back but they did not seem to bother him. Their poisonous stings would have driven us crazy, but he seemed immune. He slept like a log until Graciela woke him and we continued our conversation over cups of strong coffee.

Henry Geissler thought the possibilities for young and energetic immigrants were still as good, or possibly even better, than when he first set foot on this rich abundant soil. Coffee, sugar-cane, rice, beans, tobacco and coca thrive in the climate, and all fruit and vegetables grow faster and larger than almost anywhere else. The climate, he said, is most suitable for Europeans, in spite of what some people say. The dry season lasts from May to February and during this period it is especially profitable to plant and harvest on the large mudbanks which are entirely free from pests or plant diseases. Wild life in the jungle includes deer, armadillos, bush babies, ant-eaters, nutria, monkeys, tortoises, fish otters, giant sloths, jaguars, snakes. Fish, too, are in abundance. When the Amazon floods, however, sixty miles of the jungle on both sides of the banks go under water and nothing grows. Even fish and meat become scarce.

Geissler admitted that there were the usual tropical diseases, mainly malaria and worm conditions, but claimed they were not worse than anywhere else. As long as he was reasonably careful, Geissler seemed to think a settler here could expect less disease than he was liable to catch in Europe. But there are all sorts of small pests in the region which are most annoying. At night there are swarms of the stinging zancudos mosquitos, and during the day a small insect called pium, whose bite is most irritating and can develop into a festering sore. When swimming, one has to watch for a beautiful little fish, about a quarter of an inch long, which will try to enter any opening of the body to feed on the intestines. It has a nasty habit of entering the penis where it dies and poisons the whole body. Shoals of minute, but fierce, fish called piranhas will gnaw a human being to a skeleton within minutes if given the chance.

The local natives were charming to us and we found them friendly and quite hard-working, if not altogether reliable. Once they have worked enough to barter or buy the goods they need they disappear into the jungle and carry on their own carefree lives.

During our stay, Mrs Baxmann, a distinguished-looking Cocomilla Indian, invited us all to her home. As we sat drinking cocoa and eating cake we heard the sirens of a *lancha*, a motor freighter. Before we realised what was happening, Professor Baxmann, in shirt-sleeves and carrying his shoes and accompanied by a small Indian boy balancing a suitcase on his head, was off to board the boat with only a hurried *Adios*.

His wife explained that her husband was only going for a short trip, about five days by *lancha* to visit a business friend whose books he kept.

'He will be back in three months or so,' she said, unperturbed.

Time here has its own meaning, very different from that of civilised societies; I am quite sure it is a healthier one.

Later that afternoon we all left in my motor-boat to visit Geissler's home. He lived directly below the rapid that we had passed on our way, and since it was the dry season, a huge mudbank, cut in two by the i-ca brook, stretched in front of his fine, spacious house. Henry's wife was also Cocomilla Indian; she was now very old but must have once been very beautiful, for her strong features were still most attractive. During supper Geissler started talking, and since there seemed to be no sign of him getting tired either of us or of his own voice, Mrs Geissler picked up little Graciela, who was fast asleep in a chair, and put her to bed. Early in the morning Aenne and I were given the guest-room which was always kept in readiness for visitors.

The next day Henry began to tell us about Santa Rita do Weil. The legend of the town dates back many hundreds of years. Long ago, according to the Tucuna Indians, a Tucuna girl who had just reached the age of puberty, went to a small brook to take her ritual bath. She was never seen again and the Indians believed that a jaguar or a snake must have taken her. From then onwards the Tucunas called the brook i-ca after the name of the tree which stands on the side of the brook. They say that ever since the girl vanished a parrot has perched on the branches of the tree and that its droppings have poisoned the fish in the stream. The first white people to reach the place heard the name i-ca and made 'Rita' of it. The founding of the settlement is more recent, and is typical of many of the villages and settlements along the Amazon.

In 1870 a young German locksmith named Sebastian Weil made his way up the Amazon working at odd jobs in settlements and missions. He got a ride in one of the freight boats, which in those days were towed upstream with long ropes by gangs of Indians. At the Jesuit Mission of Santa Rita he fell in love with a Cocomilla Indian, Antonia Batalva, usually called *cabeza chata* or flat head. She was pretty, lively and intelligent and although only seventeen she was the mistress of the wealthiest man in this district, the owner of the general store in Santa Rita.

This gentleman suddenly died a mysterious death and Sebastian Weil was able to marry Antonia who had inherited her dead lover's fortune. They built themselves a large house and became still more prosperous during the rubber boom. Later, Karl Miller, a deserter from a German merchant ship, married Sebastian Weil's stepdaughter, who was the off-spring of the liaison between his wife and her rich lover. In 1905 Sebastian died mysteriously and since he was very rich, well-liked and the most respected member of the community, Santa Rita became known as Santa Rita do Weil.

Miller's marriage to Weil's stepdaughter was not a happy one. She left him for another man and took all her children and all the money with her. Five years later, when her money was gone, she returned. Miller took her back, but sent the children to be educated in Germany. Life in Santa Rita continued and several years later, during a gay party, Miller's wife again met her former lover. That night Miller, who had been ill in bed, vanished. Mrs Miller received a large life insurance payment and set up house with her former lover. Some of the descendants of Weil still live in Santa Rita but are not particularly distinguished citizens. In 1906 one of them married into the Geissler family.

By that time Santa Rita had become a trading post for the rubber collectors. There was a continuous coming and going, and one kilo of rubber was worth its weight in gold. Money was very little used in these parts and most of the trade was done in goods. Weil's store was stacked to the roof with whisky, chateaux bottled wines, champagne and the best French perfumes. Even the latest Viennese waltzes could be heard in the jungle from the recently invented gramophones that Weil sold. The rubber collectors used to arrive sick and half-starved after terrible hardships and savage fights with the Indians. Many an adventurer paid with his life for a few pounds of rubber, but those who came back had money to burn and found in Santa Rita an abundance of women, wine and food.

During those years the Amazon was heavily guarded by the Brazilians. There was a penalty of death for anyone caught

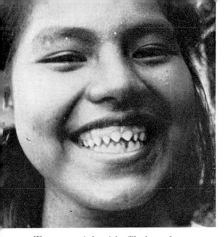

Tucuna girl with filed teeth

Nino Athayde, the Tucuna chief

*Masked Tucuna **Indians** at ritual ceremony (see page 90)*

Tucuna girl undergoing initiation ceremony (see page 92)

exporting the shoots or seeds of the wild rubber tree. Every departing ship was searched carefully but one day an English ship, filled with seeds and small plants, managed to break through. It arrived safely in London where, in great secrecy, superior strains of rubber trees were developed which became the basis for the vast plantations of the British Empire. As soon as these plantations started producing, the rubber was thrown on to the London market at an unbelievably low price and thousands of people in South America were ruined overnight. But the trading house of Weil, where young Henry Geissler worked, managed to survive.

We thought that now we had heard all there could be told about Santa Rita, but Henry insisted that the most exciting story, unknown outside Santa Rita do Weil, still had to be told.

Not far from where we were now sitting, he told us, the tragedy of the famous German explorer and ethnologist, Nimuendajú, or Curt Unckel, took place. His treatises, scientific reports and books on South America—and especially the Amazon regions—had won him the friendship and protection of the Indian general and explorer, Mariñano Candido Rondon who made him a Brazilian citizen and gave him every possible support to study the various Indian tribes of the Matto Grosso.

Nimuendajú was the first white man to tame the wild and ferocious Parintintin tribes. With eight companions he travelled in a canoe up the Amazon during the rainy season and then followed a smaller stream deep into the interior until he reached the territory of the Parintintin Indians. He found a peninsula and on it he and his companions built themselves a hut behind a barbed wire fence stretched across the peninsula. Here they lived, never leaving the hut except to go hunting and fishing for food. Several times they came across the footprints of the Indians, but never caught a glimpse of them, until one day the Indians came roaring like wild beasts out of the jungle. Nimuendajú showed himself, but immediately a rain of arrows pattered on to the metal roof of their fortress hut. The Indians continued to attack for several days, but did not dare to breach the barbed wire fence. They then tried flaming arrows, but when these

G

burned out on the tin roof, they abandoned their assault. In the lull that followed, Nimuendajú laid out presents just outside the fence. The natives gathered and looked at them with curiosity, but nothing was taken. During the next few days more and more Indians gathered and one or two of the more daring took a few things. Slowly they grew more trusting and after a month the explorer had the feared Parintintins on his side. He lived with them for six months studying their language. The Indians treated him and his companions as friends and advisors and he became very fond of them.

On his return to Manaos, Nimuendajú extracted a promise from General Rondon that none of the Parintintins would be carried off, arguing that they were not ready for civilisation. In spite of this promise another explorer visited the tribe and took half-a-dozen Indians back with him as proof of his daring exploits. These Parintintins caught every kind of disease in the superficial civilisation of Manaos, and when they returned to their homes, infected the entire tribe with syphilis. The Parintintins were disillusioned with their new friends and the religion that they had tried to impose on them. They withdrew deeper into the jungle, where they still live their old savage way of life.

Nimuendajú first went to Santa Rita do Weil in 1928 but did not contact the German settlers. He returned often to visit the Tucuna Indians and always lived in the hut of the Tucuna chief, Nino Athayde. He died on his last visit to Santa Rita in the hut of his friend, Nino. I visited Nino and accidentally discovered some pages of Nimuendajú's diary which perhaps throw some light on the causes of his sudden death.

Piecing events together from the pages, it seemed that Nimuendajú learned from Nino that the Tucuna medicine-men held an annual meeting with the medicine-men of many other tribes. This meeting took place in a large ruined temple overlooked by a giant stone god with a fantastic, demon-like head. Here were made the tribal laws, which were brutally enforced throughout the region. This was the place where war was declared and peace made; where the medicine-men decided which individuals should be punished by poisoning. New charms, new

cures, and different ways of pleasing the demon gods were discussed, and ways of enforcing discipline over the members of the
tribes decided upon.

It became Nimuendajú's most passionate wish to visit this
secret place and see it for himself. He returned again and again
to the Tucunas to try and discover the mysteries which only the
medicine-men knew. But without success as, according to their
law, every outsider who set eyes on the place would be poisoned.

Eventually Nimuendajú managed to make Nino promise to
take him to the secret meeting place and they disappeared into
the jungle. On the 10th December they returned together.
Soon afterwards when they were sitting down to supper among
Nino's family a bowl of guarapo, the juice of the sugar-cane, was
handed to Nimuendajú. As soon as he had drunk the contents he
collapsed on his hammock. The next day he was dead. It was
more than possible that the medicine-man ordered Nino to
poison Nimuendajú for having been present at their sacred
meeting.

I heard from some visiting natives that the Tucuna Indians
were going to celebrate an important ritual feast—the puberty
of a child—within the next few days. This idea fascinated me
and I pestered Henry Geissler until he said he would take us there.

We travelled by boat for two days meeting many long canoes
laden with guests going to the same celebrations. When we
arrived the feast was already in full swing. The Indians, who had
heard of our arrival, were not exactly pleased with the intrusion
and we had a noticeably cool reception. The village was some
distance from the river and as we walked along the dusty path
—passing and being passed by groups of Indians who fell into
complete silence as soon as they saw us—we felt like turning
back. Obviously we were not wanted and that was dangerous.
But the beat of the drums and the low, deep rhythm of the
chanting drew us on.

When we reached the large community hut in the village we
were pleasantly surprised to find that the father of the girl in
whose honour the feast was being held knew Geissler and
greeted us as friends. Now many of the Indians touched their

foreheads with the backs of their right hands and then let them drop slowly to touch ours. The Tucuna women brought their babies to Aenne asking her to put her hand on their foreheads as if they expected my wife to have some magic which would banish sickness from their children. Later we had to drink with them all—Aenne and Graciela included. We simply could not offend our host by refusing. Fortunately one of the drinks we had was a very pleasant wine made of fermented fruits. The women, clustering around Aenne to touch her blonde hair, had now lost their shyness and began to get cheerful and wild. To divert their attention I took some photographs. This did not surprise the Indians because Nimuendajú had taken many pictures of them.

When the sun reached the zenith, the drumming increased and movements and voices became more frenzied. The Indians were by this time more or less drunk. Suddenly, some dancing figures moved to the open space in front of the communal hut. Every one of them wore a head mask carved in soft wood depicting a ferocious demon. Tied to each of the dancers' backs was a spoked wheel covered with bark on which a human face, representing the sun, had been painted in a brownish colour. The dancers wore brightly painted materials, made of tree bark, and held long wooden spears to which dried fruits were attached and which they rattled in time to the drums. Others had wooden axes in their hands with which they tried to club the onlookers, to the joy of the entire audience. While I was trying to photograph the show I had to keep on ducking to avoid being hit. Graciela, who had never seen such fun before, did her own war-dance in an ecstasy of delight and excitement.

As suddenly as they had appeared, the dancers vanished behind the communal hut. I followed them and discovered the little girl in whose honour the festivities were taking place, hidden in a sort of seclusion chamber made of palm-leaves.

As I sat looking through the palm-leaf curtain a drove of wildly shouting and gesticulating Indians threw themselves at me. I daren't think what would have happened to me if the girl's father hadn't managed to order the warriors back to the hut.

With an angry gesture he told me to get away as no outsider was allowed to look at the girl. Before I had time to leave an axe was hurled at me by one of the masked dancers, and it was only a swift push from Geissler's friend that saved my life. I struggled up and disappeared quickly back to the communal hut where the air was thick with the smell of sweaty bodies and there was a fantastic whirling of dancers.

Then everything stopped abruptly and the middle of the hall was cleared. Now the poor little wisp of a girl, more dead than alive, was dragged in. The medicine-man danced round her and at every fourth beat of the drum he slashed a wound in her body. It was clear that every movement, every cut from the knife, was prescribed in detail by the ritual and it seemed to me that there was no sadistic emotion involved. This was an important religious ceremony and the tribe followed it with the devotion of a pious congregation. The blood that trickled out of the girl's wounds was collected in a bowl and when enough of it had been drawn, the wounds were stuck together with feathers. Afterwards the poor little girl was hardly able to stand, but seemed blissfully happy and in a trance-like state. Perhaps she was doped.

I looked for Graciela, wondering how she would be taking this strange spectacle. This was the one and only time during our journey that she seemed frightened of natives. I watched her walking about the open space, following the strange things that were being done to the little girl, forlorn and puzzled. No doubt the reason I think she was frightened this time was because she could identify herself with the girl; before, when she witnessed native rituals it had been part of the strange way that grown-ups behave.

This was the first time, too, that I found Graciela shy of the native children. She had such a great need to be with other children that this was certainly a sign of being seriously upset. Only when she was watching the dancers with their strange masks did I notice a smile on her serious little face.

Aenne's expression seemed to show a mixture of fear, disgust and sympathy for the child. She did not like watching these rites either, and was worried for Graciela. But when the women crowded round her, lifting their babies for her to bless, I saw the old sparkle of fun and amusement in her eyes as she put her hand on the children's foreheads with the pompous ceremony of a priest.

In spite of Aenne's and Graciela's discomfort I felt compelled to try and photograph the little girl, looking like a wounded bird with bloody feathers covering her body, and I asked Geissler to see if he could arrange for her to pose with Graciela. Geissler managed this very cleverly by telling the girl's father that the good demon of my tribe would feel tremendously honoured and would bring good luck and happiness to both the girls. But I had great difficulty in persuading Graciela to stand next to the blood-soaked child. Aenne pressed me to call it a day and leave the festivities, but now there was no way out. The father had been so convinced by Geissler of the beneficial results of such a picture that he was already impatiently awaiting the click of my camera.

As soon as I had finished, the girl was again brought to the middle of the hall where the magician pierced the lobes of her ears and fixed a pair of beautifully carved stone earrings. This time the strength of the dazed little creature failed. She collapsed and was carried to the seclusion chamber where her hair was cut off as a sign that she had been purged of all evil.

By late afternoon almost everyone was completely drunk. Small fights flared up and it was always the women who intervened and sent the men into the woods to sleep off the effects of the alcohol.

Things became rather difficult for us as the older women were plying us with drink from large pumpkin bowls and kept lurching towards us, almost knocking us out with their heavy-smelling breath. We were unable to hide the outbreaks of unrestrained orgies from Graciela and decided to go. At last we managed to get into my motor-boat unnoticed and steered straight for Henry's house.

During the peaceful journey downstream we talked of what we had just seen and suddenly realised that Nino, who after all was the most important chief in the district, had not been at the feast. Geissler told me that since Nimuendajú's death in 1945, Nino's position was rather strained and it looked as if he was being avoided. Was it because Nino had shown the demonic meeting-place of the medicine-men to the explorer? We decided it might be interesting to find out more about this from Nino himself. So we went as far as Henry's house and after a good night's sleep carried on up the Santa Rita river.

At that time of year the Santa Rita holds very little water and we had to travel in a narrow canoe which we often had to carry over the very shallow places. Sometimes jungle trees lay across the water and blocked our path and we had to cut our way through a maze of branches and roots. It seemed quite out of keeping to find this confusion on such a quiet-flowing river. Later we had to leave the canoe and walk for an hour along a track through thick jungle. On the way Henry stopped to show us where Nino's hut used to stand and which he had burned down immediately after Nimuendajú's death in fear of demonic retribution.

We came to Nino's new house. He was not at home, but his wife Anisia received us in front of the house with their youngest child in her arms. She was most reticent and it seemed to me as if she was afraid of us. Then Nino's daughter, Emiliana, joined our little group but she, also, seemed reserved and hardly spoke. At last Nino came home from his *roca*—the piece of jungle which he had burned down to plant maize. His wife and daughter were obviously greatly relieved when Nino arrived, but the atmosphere remained depressed. Nino brightened a little when I gave him several presents, but there was such a sinister look in his eyes when I mentioned Nimuendajú's name that I did not dare to press him further. As I felt it was hopeless to find out more without asking for serious trouble, we left the same night. All of us agreed that spending the night with the embittered Tucuna chief might be dangerous.

Back in Santa Rita do Weil Henry introduced us to two North American evangelists of the Baptist order, who had their headquarters in Benjamin Constant, not far from the Brazilian-

Peruvian-Colombian border. They were brothers and as airmen during the war had dropped bombs on Germany. The strain had made them alcoholics, until they embraced The Gospel, as they called it. They stopped drinking and became missionaries in order to make good human beings of the natives and to teach them the gospel of Christ. Both of them married healthy women, who produced healthy children, and they owned the fastest motor-boat on the river. Once every four weeks they raced upstream to Benjamin Constant. It took them four hours compared with our one week's drifting downstream. Here missionaries from the surrounding countries met to discuss policy and to gather in a prayer meeting and, last but not least, to collect their dollar cheque and to buy their canned foodstuffs.

Each of the two American brothers had built, with the help of their congregation and the labour of the Indians, a large house surrounded by a garden. In addition to the Sunday service there were evening prayers twice a week which the natives attended in moderate numbers, at the same time taking advantage of the opportunity to get medicines for their illnesses.

It was wonderful for us to enjoy a really civilised diet once more. We had North American tinned fruits, white bread and butter, apple-pie with whipped cream and iced water in coloured aluminium beakers. For little Graciela this was an exciting experience for she could hardly remember eating such delicious food. When she saw the masses of brightly-coloured plastic mechanical toys of the missionary children, she thought this was paradise, and it was heart-breaking for her to have to return to our simple life on the raft. In the end the missionaries allowed her to take three toys of her own choice to amuse her on the long journey. She chose a little clockwork ocean steamer, a small plastic fully furnished doll's house and a nurse's uniform.

Thanks to the untiring work of the missionaries almost all the Tucuna Indians have now been 'civilised'. Every one of them has been presented with a piece of clothing to hide his nakedness. Even at the heathen ceremony of the little girl's initiation almost all the Indians were partially-dressed in European garments. If a native who had been given a piece of clothing was found naked again, he would immediately lose the favour of the missionary and no more presents would be forthcoming. I don't believe that missionaries are ever able to win the hearts of the Indian tribes they try to convert. Their relationship always remains that of teacher to pupil, rich to poor, master to servant.

One interesting exception I met was a woman missionary. This young German, who belonged to a special sect, had pirated many souls from the land 'civilised' by the Salesiana Missions. She preached that the end of the world was close at hand, working was useless, and that the only salvation was to prepare oneself for the impending doom by the singing of religious hymns. She drummed these hymns into the Indians who, using their primitive instruments as accompaniment, responded with genuine enthusiasm. But mainly, I think, because they love music.

The word of this wonderful new religion spread through the jungle and the lady missionary soon had a vast following. The result for the Catholic mission was appalling. Not only did they lose most of their followers, but they also could not find anyone to work for them.

The day of our departure from Santa Rita do Weil had to come and we bade farewell to the good missionaries, who in their generosity had equipped us with a store of delicacies, like tins of food and white flour. Old Geissler looked sad and philosophical as we promised to return and listen to more of his stories; perhaps he felt that he would never again find such good listeners.

I cast off the rope and we slowly drifted past the little village. When Graciela lost sight of the missionary children who had assembled to wave to her, she turned thoughtfully to her play-corner on the raft to arrange her new toys amongst the crudely carved native figures, hollowed-out fruits, coloured stones and the shrunken head of a child.

8

Goodbye to the Raft

AFTER drifting for a day and a night from Santa Rita do Weil, we tied up the next afternoon at San Pablo de Olivensa. This is the main village of the upper Amazon and has a Mayor and representatives of all political parties.

Just as we had made our cumbersome craft safe on the river bank, a heavy thunderstorm worked upstream. All the motor-launches cast off and set off to ride out the turmoil in the middle of the stream. For us this was out of the question as it would have taken far too long to get moving, so, using extra ropes, I tied up the raft as firmly as I could.

Meanwhile black clouds had gathered immediately above us and darkness was over the river. The crews of the local ships shook their heads sadly and it was obvious that they already imagined our crushed raft disintegrating in the waves. The storm rushed at us with such force that it took our breath away. I felt the rain penetrating my shirt like the lash of a whip, but Aenne and I had no time for reflection. We were kept running desperately hither and thither with wooden buffers trying to cushion the raft as it was tossed against the steep river bank. Our poor home groaned and creaked in agony, but the logs, so ingeniously lashed together by the Indians, withstood the strain. Waves washed over us, but the mooring ropes held and whenever one of the stakes which anchored them to the ground worked loose, I jumped out and drove in another.

The thunderstorm disappeared upriver as suddenly as it had arrived; I found my bottle of sugar-cane schnapps and took a well-deserved drink. The captain of a *lancha* asked me to join him in a bottle of whisky to celebrate our survival; he thought it incredible that we had managed to navigate the raft all this way without an accident. Coming from an old Amazon expert, this made me feel very proud and, in retrospect, rather frightened. But he warned me that the storms would become even more dangerous. Lower down, he said, large rivers joined the Amazon swelling it to many times its present size; he advised me to keep continuous watch for thunderclouds and to remain close to the left bank so that I could find protection in good time.

Otherwise, San Pablo brought us luck. A wild and rather alcoholic election campaign was being fought; speakers were flown in and *lanchas* arrived full of beer. There were brass bands, picnics, dances and mass meetings. Everyone was determined to enjoy the election and I was kept busy day and night taking photographs, developing and making prints. Our raft was overrun by politicians who could not wait to see themselves in black and white. So, once more, we had some cash to replenish our stores and buy petrol.

Just as we were leaving, Graciela discovered a little ant-eater sitting on the shoulder of an Indian. She shouted and performed such a crazy war-dance that at first we thought she must have hurt her foot. When we learned what it was all about we managed to buy the animal from the Indian. He was soon at home with us and climbed all over the verandah. For the first few days the five parakeets made terrible noises of protest, but they soon got used to the new arrival. He slept all day, but after sunset he became lively, jumping and climbing about. He seemed to enjoy swinging close to the sleeping birds who awoke in a horrible temper, squawking noisily. The little bear was not at all disturbed by the outcry and went on hunting for insects; as there were none inside the mosquito wire, we put him on the roof where he was busy all night.

On our first morning we found a woodpecker sitting on a drifting log in the middle of the river. His head plumes were cardinal red and the rest of him a deep black. He seemed exhausted, but he defended himself bravely until I eventually caught him and added him to our menagerie on the verandah. He recovered by the evening and became a delightful companion.

We had lots of fun with our small passengers. The little bear would tumble about and look at us thoughtfully with his beady eyes, the woodpecker gave us a staccato concert, pecking away at the corner-post of our verandah, the coloured parakeets climbed about the mosquito wire babbling the new words they had learned. Like this we drifted peacefully through the jungle, listening to its strange noises. Nature was so peaceful on this stretch of the river that we allowed ourselves to be carried along into the darkness of the night. Suddenly there was a jolt. The raft had drifted on to a sandbank. It was completely dark and there was nothing I could do until the next morning. At sunrise we jumped into the water and struggled and heaved to free the raft. Once we were afloat again I had to probe the depths for hours to get back into the right channel. Some way downstream we saw a small wooden shack belonging to some Caboclos, a hybrid race of Indians and Negroes. There were beautiful water-melons and young maize on their plantation, but they were too lazy to get them for us. Some schnapps and tobacco eventually gave them sufficient encouragement to trade with us and we bought thirty very tasty melons and a hundred corn cobs.

That evening we reached the Putumayo, a river which flows from Colombia and is navigable as far as the Andes.

When we continued our journey next morning, we had, for the first time, a really effective following wind. Our hut acted as a sail and we overtook the waves. The river had become very wide, like a sea between the jungle, with not a single settlement in view. In the afternoon the usual thunderstorm approached, but we did not know where it would break and we took the pre-caution of pulling the raft into the left bank with the motor-boat. Down-river the storm had already started and we could see the waves foaming towards us. We were suddenly enveloped in a blinding wall of whirling sand and then all hell broke loose. But we survived. We were becoming increasingly efficient in handling the raft in emergencies and we were slowly shaping into an experienced Amazon crew.

Whenever the weather was rough or we had to battle with the river, things were tough for Graciela and Aenne. I had to leave them to struggle on their own while I jumped into the motor-boat and manoeuvred the raft to safety. They could see me yelling instructions to them, but the sounds were drowned by the noise of the rain and storm. Neither of them could swim and Aenne continually worried about what would happen if ever I was sick or injured. So during calm periods I tried to teach her how to steer the raft. When I began showing her how to handle the motor-boat, the engine kicked back as she was starting it. She strained her wrist and from that day on she was more scared of the motor than of cannibals!

During the quiet spells when the tropical sun was reflected in the water, my wife and child were happy and contented. At those times life for Graciela was not so different from that of other children brought up in isolated places. Apart from lessons in reading, writing and arithmetic, she had several household tasks to keep her busy. She had to feed and clean her animals, and it was also her job to sweep the deck and help Aenne dry the dishes. When her mother did not pester her with jobs she was at her busiest. Her favourite occupation was making dolls' clothes. Aenne did the cutting and Graciela sewed with passionate determination. Usually the pieces of material available were not large enough for a big doll, so Graciela simply sewed together all sorts of pieces of every colour and texture until she had a length of cloth suitable to be cut into a dress. Unfortunately she didn't have a large doll, but she was quite happy completing a wardrobe of a dozen dresses in the confidence that one day she would have one.

Learning for Graciela was a much slower process than making clothes for imaginary dolls. She liked arithmetic, and it is still her best subject, but at first she could make little progress in reading and writing. I am sure it would have been very much less of a struggle both for Aenne and Graciela if there had been other children to learn with. As it was poor Graciela was always alone, and with all the interesting things continuously passing in front of her eyes, it was hard for her to get to grips with the cold letters of the alphabet.

As we drifted on the Amazon became wider and wider. Storms became more frequent and violent and kept us on our toes. Time passed quickly as we travelled on, passing Porto Alfonso and heading towards Manaos where the Rio Negro flows into the Amazon. We had done six hundred and eighty-five hours' drifting time since we left Pucallpa and the strain was beginning to tell. I found it difficult to sleep, and when I did I dreamed that the raft had torn itself free from its moorings. Rather than lie awake worrying I would get up, cast off and let ourselves drift on through the night.

Finally we reached the mouth of the Rio Negro where the water was coal black, like its name, but, unlike the brown clay waters of the Amazon, crystal clear.

Manaos lies a short way up the Rio Negro, and I tried to tow the raft upstream to it. But we did not cover more than a hundred yards in two hours and I had to find some other method. After several unsuccessful appeals for help, we found a launch to take us in tow. This cost me a small fortune and left us completely broke. Four hours later we reached the harbour of Manaos where, like a floating village, hundreds of houseboats were anchored.

Manaos is a small town surrounded by the largest jungle in the world. It has a monumental opera house built of Italian marble as a reminder of its days of glory during the rubber boom. An antiquated tram-line still runs along the streets and takes passengers to the edge of the jungle. The streets are beautifully paved in coloured mosaics, but near the outskirts of the town the jungle has advanced relentlessly while the local people wait passively for the return of the golden days of the rubber boom.

My most urgent problem was to make money, so I called at the Chamber of Commerce and asked the president about the possibility of staging an exhibition. Half-an-hour later I left with the building's marble hall at my disposal. Within a few days three hundred of my photographs and trophies, including the shrunken heads, were on view, and since it was free my exhibition attracted a great number of visitors. I fixed a little box at the exit so that anyone who wanted to could put money in it. There was a depression in Manaos at the time and many people were living on credit, but I collected an appreciable sum.

Again and again I was stopped by old-timers of the jungle and told of the gruesome, but glorious, days of the rubber boom. Some tore open their shirts to show the scars from the arrows, and many told me tales of savage fights with the Indians of the interior. When we dismantled the exhibits the Chamber of Commerce presented us with a few thousand cruzeiros and wished us luck for the remainder of our journey.

We were at last in a place where we could buy Graciela a doll for the home-made trousseau. We did not take her with us to buy it as we had a shrewd idea that the local shops would not have one up to the standards of her dreams. We were right, so we bought the best we could. When we gave it to her she burst into tears of disappointment. It was definitely not *her* doll. But once she realised she had no alternative, she adapted herself to the circumstances with the logic of her nine years and was blissfully happy with her dream substitute.

Manaos represents another cornerstone in Graciela's life as it was the place where she wrote her first letter—to her grandmother in Germany. It was a struggle and cost Aenne almost as much in self-control and nervous energy as all the rapids put together. In the end I think Aenne was prouder of the letter than Graciela.

I decided to get some official information from the Brazilian Border Commission about the next stage of our journey to the Casiquiare—the watershed that connects the Rio Negro with the Orinoco. The commission knew nothing of this route and could not even tell me if it was navigable. So I called on the school of the Salesiana Brethren where I met a monk who knew the district. But this visit was no more reassuring. He told me that many travellers had been lost and never seen again in the labyrinth of thousands of islands and said that no one could navigate the Rio Negro without a pilot. He also warned me of rapids and underwater roots and of places where we would have to drag our craft overland. We could not avoid dangerous tribes, some of them cannibals who might as well be living in the Stone Age. He could give me no information about the watershed by which we hoped to reach the Orinoco, and in general thought my plan to get from the Rio Negro into the Orinoco and from there to the Caribbean sea entirely unrealistic.

The sensible thing would be to go on drifting down the Amazon on our comfortable raft until we reached the Atlantic. But this no longer appealed to me. The Amazon now would be busy with *lanchas*, steamers and freight-carrying rafts. Villages and settlements would be more numerous and the closer we got to the Atlantic the more civilised and dull would be our surroundings. I was not yet ready for civilisation and I had not had my fill of the jungle.

To leave the Amazon would mean changing over from our comfortable raft to the motor-boat and from what the monk told me I knew it would be a dangerous trip.

Thinking about the alternatives I wondered whether to send Graciela and Aenne to Caracas, while I continued up the Rio Negro and on to the Caribbean alone. But when I suggested this to Aenne she would have none of it. She intended to go with me and that, of course, meant Graciela as well.

So we sold the raft which had served us so faithfully. It was bought by a Caboclo who wanted to make a floating liquor shack of it. To be drowned in liquor rather than in the muddy waters of the Amazon was a pleasant prospect for any old-timer, and we felt quite happy with the fate of our old friend. We often wonder how it is faring now.

We now set out on the long journey up the Rio Negro with our motor-boat overloaded with two tons of luggage and provisions. We had stacked a row of petrol cans on the roof, but these made the boat top-heavy and forced us to make an emergency landing after only a few minutes. All the cans had to be stowed inside the boat which lay only a foot above the water. Fortunately the Rio Negro was like a millpond and we made some progress. At midday we ran into a thunderstorm and were forced to make a second emergency landing. For a moment the situation was desperate. We would have sunk had we not thrown everything we could spare overboard, including the car battery which I needed for my enlarger. Even then the boat was so overcrowded that I could hardly get from the wheel in the bows to the motor controls in the stern.

On our first night I had a battle with Graciela over the best sleeping quarters. In the end her ladyship won, as could be expected. The corners and sharp edges of boxes, fishing rods and

On the way to the
Cauabury tribe

Yagua village (*see page* 75)

Cauabury archer

tents dug into my ribs while Graciela slept peacefully surrounded by her prize possessions in the middle of the boat.

From then on we decided to spend the nights on the river bank and for the first time in years we had the pleasure of sleeping in the open without being confined in mosquito nets. For Aenne these nights were torture. The creaking and rustling from the undergrowth and the cries of the animals terrified her, but I just could not keep my eyes open to reassure her.

Graciela was seldom frightened of the beasts of the jungle or the natives. She only feared the giant palms whose heavy crowns swayed in the breeze. Some of these giants had crashed into the water close by us during the storms on the Amazon and Graciela had never forgotten it. 'If one of those trees falls on my head, I shall be dead,' she used to say before going to sleep. To soothe her I would tell her of the hundreds of long roots which held the trees so that they could embrace each other firmly and lean together whispering secrets. This story calmed her and sent her peacefully to sleep.

Later we all came to love those nights under the open sky and we looked forward to our bonfire and the simple meal we would cook over it. Aenne had learned to prepare a crisp, dry rice and with it we had turtle meat or turtle eggs. There was not so much fruit here as on the Amazon and our main food, apart from rice, was corn-meal. When we had eaten we would tie our hammocks to palm-trees and sleep peacefully and happily.

What impressed us at first was the fact that the Rio Negro really is black. This is caused by the dissolved roots of a variety of mango-tree which also destroys the larvae of the fever-carrying mosquito, making the area almost mosquito free.

When we arrived at Barcelos, the first missionary settlement on the Rio Negro, neither Aenne nor Graciela had a decent dress to wear and had to go visiting in rough trousers and open-necked shirts. Graciela longed to be dressed like the girls of the mission school with whom she immediately made friends. She told the Mother Superior that she wanted to go to church like the other girls, but thought it would be disrespectful in her long pants. Two days later she was presented with a sweet little dress and

H

underwear which had been sewn for her by the girls of the mission. From then on she made a special point of visiting the Mother Superior the moment we arrived at a mission settlement.

All this time we had been dragging Graciela's bicycle round with us. I had often tried to get rid of this cumbersome piece of luggage, especially after we left the raft. But Graciela watched it like a hawk and cried whenever we mentioned the possibility of leaving it behind. She felt that the bicycle gave her status when she arrived at the jungle stations, shabby and with few belongings. None of the other little boys and girls in the mission schools had ever seen such a machine before and were impressed by Graciela's skill in riding it. When the Indian children could spare time from their lessons, Graciela tried to teach them how to cycle. She was very happy in these mission schools and would have liked to stay in one if only Aenne and I could stay too.

For the next eight days we did not meet a single living being. This was the most lovely river we had travelled so far. Its crystal-clear black waters reflected the lush green scenery with exagger-ated intensity and there was something eerie about its blackness and the deep silence which seemed to engulf us, making us nervously watchful.

Several times we lost our way in innumerable river-arms and often found ourselves at a dead end. Sometimes it was days before we again found the right stream. One day, like a mirage, we noticed movement on the water and after a moment saw white, gleaming foam dripping from oars as they dipped regularly into the black water. For the first time in days the stillness of the river was broken by the rhythmic splashing of paddles. The dugout pushed straight toward us. At last we would be able to check our position and find out how far it was to the next inhabited place. Then the splashing stopped abruptly, the canoe turned round and vanished into the distance. As soon as it was out of sight the loneliness once more seemed complete and we could not imagine that only a few minutes ago there had been other human beings sharing the river with us.

Shortly afterwards a blinding flash, accompanied by crashing thunder, disturbed the stillness again. A black storm-cloud swooped down on us, turning in ever faster and closer circles like a spinning top until it hit the river and greedily sucked masses of foaming water into the air. It is said that complete shoals of fish have been sucked up like this and deposited many miles away. Further on, where the sky was still blue, a wall of yellow sand rose slowly into the sky and daylight changed into darkness. Only the white gleaming crowns of the black waves gave us any light. With all its force the storm cloud threw itself against the noisily protesting jungle, uprooting giant trees and cutting a straight path of destruction through its tangled growth as far as the eye could see. I still can't explain how I managed to keep our overloaded boat from being swamped.

One evening we reached a leper colony. The lepers told us that they had escaped from one of the large settlements near Manaos some years before to live their lives away from civilisation and interference. Their sole income came from the sale of dried fish which they took, every few months, to the market in Manaos. During the night an intense rushing sound like a waterfall awoke us. We were told that this was caused by large shoals of fish searching for breeding grounds.

We had now reached the mouth of the Rio Branco, the white river. From here the north bank of the Rio Negro was terrorised by the most ferocious Indian tribes. Settlers who had prospered in the region had been forced to leave the river bank because of the continuous raids by these savage Indians. They attacked the settlements, killing the men, capturing the women and children, and burning the houses to the ground.

I have only heard of one woman—Luciana Venceslau Candido —who managed to escape from them. She lived with her husband Feliciando Candido, two children and some relatives on an isolated farm by the river. One evening at dusk the farm was attacked by a horde of the Cauabury Indians. A hail of arrows overtook the family as they tried to escape into the jungle. Signora Candido, carrying her two-year-old baby in her arms and dragging her five-year-old son behind her, followed her husband as fast as she could. A poisoned arrow pierced the heart of her baby, and the mother, overcome by grief, gave up and was taken prisoner with her elder child. They tramped through the jungle with the tribe for six days until they reached a native village where they were kept prisoners for many months. But one night during a feast when the entire tribe was drunk, Signora Candido escaped with her son. For weeks mother and son wandered through the jungle until they met some half-civilised Indians who took them to Manaos.

Even without the Cauabury menace it would be difficult to settle in this area as, during the rainy season, the river floods up to a width of one hundred and fifty miles in places.

After weeks of travel and battling with thunderstorms we reached a point where the river has to force its way through a hundred-yard-wide gulley. This is the beginning of a series of frightening rapids ending at Santa Isabel. Each day we struggled with a new obstacle, but, stage by stage, we fought our way upriver. Our nerves, already tense from the storms, could hardly stand the strain of the new hardships as we were thrown about helplessly in the boiling whirl of the water. But luck, or perhaps a newly-developed second sense showed us the right channel. When we learned that even the Indians never navigate these parts without a pilot born and bred on the river, we felt proud of ourselves.

At last the Rio Negro became peaceful again and we could enjoy the dreamlike scenery. Thousands of brightly-coloured parakeets fluttered over the white sandbanks which gleamed against the black waters of the river. Jungle trees decked with a variety of blooming orchids were mirrored in the water.

We decided to rest at the mouth of the Rio Cauabury. There was little water in the river in the dry season and we easily found a nice flat rock with a soft sandbank spread in front of it. Graciela was eager to get out of the cramped boat and the prospect of a few days on land thrilled her at least as much as the prospect of a summer holiday in the country would excite a city child. Her greatest pleasure was looking for turtle eggs. There were masses buried in the sand and she seemed to have a second sense in knowing exactly where to dig. During the moonless nights thousands of turtles clamber cumbersomely from the river on to the sandbanks where they dig holes and lay thirty to forty eggs in each, before covering them laboriously with sand. After dark

Rio Negro

Wooden fire-lighter

Cañamuda, the plant that paralyses the tongue (see page 130)

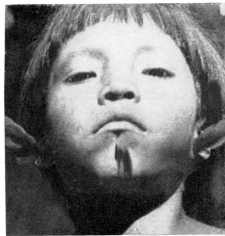

Cauabury Indian boy

Hard-wood arrows and spears, N.W. Brazil

pumas, jaguars and snakes search the sandbanks for the fresh
eggs, so we were not alone any longer at night. Graciela and I
did not mind the company, but Aenne was nervous. She did not
like it when the two of us fell asleep while she was listening to
the jungle noises and imagining us threatened by wild beasts.

A few days after our arrival I noticed human footprints on
our sandbank and on closer inspection I found they had been
made recently. I now remembered the empty huts we had seen
on the bank and wondered if the inhabitants had been wiped
out by the feared Cauabury tribe. I did not tell my wife about
my discovery but decided to camp on the other side of the black
river from then on. I also found the recent track of a tapir which
must have been the size of a fat calf. Indian, or no Indian, I
could not resist the temptation so I took my old shot gun and went
after it. I was carefully looking for the tapir tracks when I noticed
another fresh imprint of a human foot. Alarmed, I broke into a
run with the idea of getting to my family on the open sandbank.
Somehow I had a feeling that we were in mortal danger.

On the edge of the jungle I tripped over something and fell
head-first into a wild bamboo thicket. A bamboo thorn entered
my left arm and the sudden biting pain made me cry out. I
calmed myself and tried to extract the thorn, but it broke and
the tip lodged in the flesh. There was nothing else for it but to
get back as quickly as possible. But when I tried to avoid the
object over which I had stumbled, I realised that it was the body
of a native, naked except for a ribbon with bunches of coloured
ara feathers on one arm. A piece of string was tied round his
abdomen and to this was attached the tip of his penis.

These were the unmistakable signs of the Cauabury tribe. I
wondered if the Indian was alone or if he had friends in the
vicinity. I examined the man and found there was a little life
in the body. His foot was blue and bloated, and poison had
obviously affected his entire body. A six-foot bow and a dozen
arrows were scattered around him and close by I discovered a
dead snake measuring five feet. It was a jergon snake, the rarest
and most poisonous snake in South America. It has a head as big
as a bulldog and long sharp teeth. This snake attacks by jumping

often a distance of up to fifteen feet, to dig its poisonous teeth into its victim's flesh. Without a special serum a victim will die a most painful death. There was little doubt that the native had been bitten by the snake, but had had time to kill it before he lost consciousness.

Just then the Indian twitched in horrible convulsions and I realised that there was more life in him than I had thought. I rushed off back to the sandbank, fetched some serum from the boat and returned and gave a shot to the Indian. When he did not move after ten minutes, I emptied another phial into him. In spite of the fact that his skin had turned a deep blue-green and he looked as if he were dead, I then got Aenne to help me drag his heavy body to the sandbank where we received non-stop advice and questions from Graciela. Slowly the horrible colour of the Indian's skin turned to a light red and he began to moan quietly. Watching him as he struggled to keep alive I reflected that only an hour ago he was ready to kill me and that it was likely that one of the most dangerous snakes in South America had saved my life. But most of my thoughts were bent on medical speculations. I calculated that we were only ten hours away from a missionary settlement on the upper Rio Negro and it was probable we would find a doctor there.

I started the motor and we went full speed upstream. Our progress was slow because the current was getting strong and when I tried to increase the revolutions of the engine the overheated exhaust pipe glowed red. This gave me a fright. Close by were several petrol containers, some of which were leaking badly, filling the boat with fumes. There was no time to spare for repairs, nor could we afford to throw the leaking petrol cans overboard. We shifted Graciela and our most precious belongings aft and prayed that the boat would not blow up. We had no alternative if we wanted to save the Indian's life. This was my big chance. If I could make friends with this cannibal of the Cauabury tribe, a relationship which no white man had yet achieved, I might find a way of visiting these most primitive and ferocious of all South American peoples.

In spite of the rapids and the leaking petrol cans, we reached the missionary settlement safely. For five days the Indian fought death.

The colour of his skin changed daily, and his convulsions became less intense as the days went by. On the fifth day the colour of his body changed to a bluish-black, but from then on he improved steadily. A few days later he awoke for the first time, bathed in sweat. He looked about with animal fear in his eyes. Luckily the doctor and I were present, otherwise he would have fallen out of his hammock in his desperate struggle to escape. Only after fifteen minutes did he give up and fall into a deep exhausted sleep.

From then on we made sure that he was always carefully guarded because he made wild and sudden attempts to escape. As guards we chose friendly Indians of various tribes until we found a Macu Indian who succeeded in making himself understood to the Cauabury. We discovered his name was Waraeki and he lived with his tribal brothers near the upper reaches of the Cauabury river. After a few weeks Waraeki had completely recovered and we had managed to learn a few Cauabury words. Waraeki, too, had picked up a few Portuguese words and we were able to understand each other quite well. I started to cultivate Waraeki's friendship which was not too difficult since he understood I had saved his life, but he was so overwhelmed by his surroundings that it took him some time to lose his fear and suspicion. Only when we went hunting together did he open up and act naturally, as this was something he had experienced before and in which he excelled. Whenever he came with me we bagged at least twice as much as when I was alone. Not the faintest animal trail escaped his trained eyes and he was able to copy every animal sound perfectly—so perfectly that we never failed to get an answer. The jungle, otherwise dead and still during the day, suddenly began to live in Waraeki's presence.

Finally, I felt sufficiently sure of his friendship to send him back to his tribe. I made him understand that I wished him to return after he had told his people that we wished to visit them and that our intentions were friendly.

Waraeki left us, happily smiling and loaded with gifts, and the sparkle of his big black eyes assured me that he would return soon to lead Aenne, Graciela and myself to a place never before visited by white people.

9

The Demon Flute

IT was well over a month before Waraeki returned. I was
immediately faced with a difficult decision. As an old vagabond I did not hesitate to accept Waraeki's invitation to visit
his scarcely-known tribe. They had the reputation of being on
the warpath with practically every tribe in the region. Other
Indians called them robbers of women, or eaters of human flesh,
and the very name Cauabury was enough to terrify them. The
responsibility of taking my wife and child to stay with these
savages worried me, but as usual, I decided to trust to luck.
After all, I rationalised, I have had better experiences with completely primitive people than with half-civilised natives corrupted
and demoralised by our so-called civilisation. The presence of my
wife and little girl always had a friendly and pacifying influence
on genuine primitive people; they were better protection than
any shotgun or revolver.

Waraeki had brought back a friend with him and they told
us that they were going to take us by boat up the Cauabury
River since the overland route was far too dangerous and tiring
for Aenne and Graciela. It was quite out of the question to take
the motor-boat through the numerous rapids that we would
encounter so one morning at sunrise we left in a heavy native
dugout. Waraeki paddled at the bow and his friend at the stern,
while we sat in the middle under the shade of a banana-leaf roof.
It would have been a romantic voyage, had it not been for the
many interruptions when the canoe had to be dragged and
pushed overland to bypass the rapids. Slowly the mountains
became closer and the river ran faster, becoming more and more

difficult to navigate. Minute mosquitos, called piums, almost drove us mad in spite of the mosquito oil which we rubbed on continuously.

One day, two weeks after we had left, we turned towards the bank and before the boat touched we saw a group of naked people, full of friendly smiles, waiting for us. This was the Cauabury settlement and Waraeki's home and it was obvious that he had spoken well of us. The women remained in the background, the men at a fair distance, but the children, as always, trusting and a little cheeky, rushed down the river-bank to meet us. Then Waraeki led me to a group of men who made guttural sounds obviously intended to convey formal greetings. A few feet from them I bowed respectfully and greeted them as well as I could. Graciela who had followed me, spoiled the dignified ceremony by pulling my shirt-sleeves and plying me with questions. Neither the Cauaburys nor I understood each other's language, but there was little doubt in my mind that we understood each other's friendly feelings. Now my wife and Waraeki joined us and led by the reception committee, we set off in single file along the path to the village, the chattering women and children following.

After a mile or so we reached a hut which consisted of a palm-leaf roof on thin poles with walls of woven matting, enclosing a large almost empty room. Hammocks made of fibres of the tuca palm-tree were strung between poles; on the open side of the hut a small fireplace was glowing. Waraeki now untied the hammocks from the poles, pushed out the old woman with a little girl who had been living there, and gave us to understand that this would be our home. Walking back to our canoe to fetch our belongings I noticed with great relief that the plague of mosquitos had diminished greatly as soon as we had left the river. When we returned to the hut the crowd of Indians, who had been standing around it, had vanished and Aenne and Graciela sat peacefully in front of the fire making coffee.

The next morning Graciela found herself three playmates, three little naked boys between seven and nine years old. They watched her with wide open eyes as she drew large squares in the sand, and proceeded to jump from one to another pushing a stone in front of her. When she was bored with playing by herself she pulled one of the little boys into a square and showed him with unmistakable gestures what it was all about. It was not long before all three were playing together as if they had known each other all their lives. When I looked out for them again the group had grown considerably—and it appeared that all the cannibal children in the settlement had allowed themselves to be organised into two bands for a most realistic game of cowboys and Indians. Graciela, her cheeks flushed bright red, her blonde hair tousled and sticking to her forehead, stood in the centre of the naked and admiring little band giving orders with the grand gestures of a general.

The Cauabury children treated our little daughter as a goddess suddenly fallen from heaven to teach them how to play. They satisfied instantly every one of her wishes and it was amazing how quickly she managed to convey to them what she wanted. But soon power corrupted her and when the children did not understand immediately what she wanted, she lost her temper and pushed them about. Never once did I see any of the children try to defend themselves. The most they did was to duck out of the fury of their goddess. They never tired of admiring her fair hair and light skin, but most of all they loved the games she taught them. Slowly a kind of rivalry developed amongst the boys who brought their bows and arrows and their blowpipes to Graciela and had competitions to show her who was the most skilful. Graciela was most impressed and showed her pleasure with loud bursts of laughter. For her it was paradise.

On the first day she asked me why all the boys had a shaved tonsure on their heads. I had already noticed that Waraeki had a large round bald spot on his crown, very much like a monk, except that the spot was painted bright red. I told Graciela for fun that the cannibals had once caught a monk who had tasted so delicious that they decided to adopt the hairstyle in his honour! She looked at me thoughtfully, but could not understand why her little playmates were so partial to human flesh. Then she wanted to know why they painted the bald patch with red paint, but luckily Waraeki arrived and spared me an answer. He came to take me to the village about two hundred yards away. The Cauaburys, I discovered, did not live in large community huts like the Macus, each family having its own hut. The huts were built in a large semicircle and were almost identical with the palm-leaf roofs high in front and sloping right to the ground at the back. The huts were empty except for the fireplaces and the hammocks tied between the poles that held up the roofs. As Waraeki and I walked round the settlement, the women and children squatting on the hard, clay floors looked at us with empty animal-like stares. The toddlers hid themselves behind their mothers or began to scream. They behaved quite differently from the jolly natural way in which they had greeted us. Not a man was in sight and I wondered whether they were holding a meeting somewhere to decide our future. After this rather puzzling visit I returned to our hut. Night was falling quickly and there was nothing for us to do but crawl into our hammocks for our first night in the midst of the cannibals.

The next morning, before it was quite light, I made my way to a little stream behind our hut to fetch water for our coffee. On the way I met the whole village walking in single file to the river to take a bath. The men led the way and went into the water first. They splashed about ducking their heads under, and brushing their teeth with clay smeared on one finger, then rinsing their mouths. Back on land they wiped the water from their bodies with their hands. In the meantime the women and children arrived at the river, making a great deal more noise and commotion. The children had great fun ducking and splashing each other and even the smallest swam, using a doglike stroke to keep afloat.

While the women were bathing the men painted themselves with a red juice from the urucu plant. Each one of them drew different designs on his face and body, taking great pains over the job. One painted thin lines from his upper lip to his nose and from there across his cheeks. Another covered his nose and chin with an unpleasant-smelling blue paint. Every colour and design has its significance, and was strictly related to the special task or work that the Indian would be doing that day. The results looked fantastic and would have terrified any uninitiated stranger.

Waraeki joined me on the beach, and although I knew that Aenne would be waiting impatiently for the water, I could not drag myself away from this lively scene. Waraeki told me that the men would now be going hunting and that there were plenty of tapirs, wild pigs and monkeys in the locality. As I watched, the natives grabbed their bows and bundles of long arrows and vanished into the jungle.

Almost every arrow had a different type of point, some were like flat-pointed spoons, others had hooks and some had smooth tips with two or three rings carved into the point. These are the dreaded poisoned arrows which leave the poison in the wound when the arrow is removed.

After the women and children had finished their morning bath they walked to the nearby plantation to start work. Together with Waraeki I accompanied them, forgetting all about my poor wife and her coffee. The women tended patches of yuca, a species of potato root. Maize and bananas were also grown. Waraeki told me that there was never any stealing as this was punishable by death, but murder of any person not belonging to the tribe was condoned, if not welcomed.

Aenne had become restless by the time I returned and made me feel a thoughtless brute. After some time Graciela's playmates arrived and a little later Waraeki fetched me to shoot fish in the river. We climbed into his dugout and paddled to the first rapid where we anchored the boat. Waraeki posted himself at the bow, standing upright and holding a spear above his head, while I sat astern with a small bow and arrow at the ready. The arrow had three hooks at its point and was used for shooting smaller fish. I was too fascinated by the beautiful figure and poise of Waraeki as he stood motionless staring into the water to pay much attention to the fish. He was about five foot four inches tall, the average height for his tribe and his body was perfectly proportioned. Cauaburys are easily amongst the best-looking primitive Indians I met.

The sun beat down remorselessly on the clear green river and

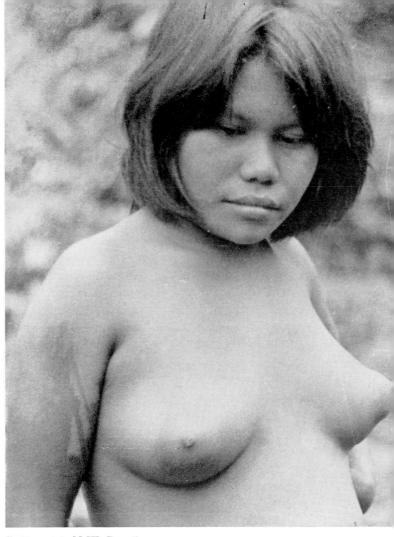

Indian girl, N.W. Brazil

Medicine-man treating sick Indian

Young Tucano mother

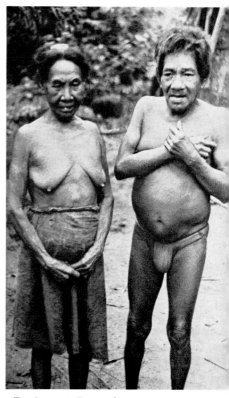

Darby and Joan of the upper Rio Negro

in spite of the rushing, cool-looking waters, it was terribly hot. But Waraeki stood motionless, seemingly for ever, until quite suddenly his spear swished into the water. Within seconds a huge fish jumped into the air only to fall back into the water with a clumsy splash. The line fixed to the spear raced out, Waraeki grabbed it, pulled in the fish and hit it on the head with a club. A few tremors and lashes from its tail and the huge zungarro lay still in the dugout. It was a wonderful fish weighing at least forty pounds. We had done our day's work and went home.

We left a piece of fish with my wife and then continued to the village. By now the sun was beginning to go down and the men had returned from hunting and the women from the fields. Each man handed his catch to his woman, who stuck it on a wooden spear which she rammed into the ground close to a roaring fire so that the heat slowly cooked the meat. The skin and fur were left on. When the animal had cooked sufficiently in its own juice the head of the family skinned it and distributed chunks of meat to his various relatives, taking good care that the men were served with the choice pieces first. Roasted corn cobs and green bananas were also eaten. Only when the men had finished were the women and children allowed to eat. The Cauaburys did not seem to know of salt and simply put a pinch of ash on to each piece of meat before eating it. Nor did they know of cooking in pots and always roasted their vegetables and meat on the open fire.

On my way home I watched two families walking in single file from opposite directions greeting each other. The men walked ahead. Behind them came the boys, then the girls and, lastly, the women carrying their babies. The men of both families met each other, stopped and began talking. The women and children remained silently watching at some distance, not daring to interrupt. The women are in every way the slaves of the Cauabury men. They perform all the heavy work in the fields and, supervised by the men, they carry huge baskets on their backs tied with a sling to their foreheads, usually nursing a baby at the same time. The women also fetch the water which they carry in dried pumpkin shells balanced on their heads. The young girls move gracefully and have the perfect figures and beautiful breasts which one finds only in primitive people. It is considered unworthy for any man to carry anything other than his hunting-gear.

The next day the tribe celebrated a minor feast, to which Waraeki invited me. I could make myself understood only with signs and drawings in the sand, but since Indians have the inborn patience of angels we managed to communicate successfully. The feast was arranged in honour of a ten-year-old girl who had had her first menstruation not long before and who had since lived isolated with an old woman in the hut which we now occupied. During this time all the men of the tribe avoided the pair and the girl lived on a prescribed diet. She was taught the facts of life by the old woman and advised how best to please men. She was also taught how to work efficiently and how to keep house for her future husband. When we arrived the tuition of the girl had just been completed and the parents had arranged this drinking party in honour of their daughter's coming of age. At sundown we all went to the hut of the parents where the girl had been all day, watched over by the old woman. The first act of the ceremony was performed by the medicine-man who shaved the hair from the girl's head and burned it while solemnly mumbling magic spells. Then he took the ashes and gave them to the girl. At midnight she took them to the river, where I secretly watched her scatter them in the water. After that she took a bath and returned to the hut. Waraeki told me later that the purpose of this ceremony was to drive away the evil spirits from the body of the girl. Next morning she was allowed to eat normal food again, but was kept in the hut for several more days. After that she was ready to marry. We celebrated all night and I returned to our hut with a splitting headache and feeling nauseated. Aenne and Graciela felt anything but sorry for me. They had been terrified by the slow, deep rhythm of the drums and the rustlings in the bushes and throaty shrieks and yells from the celebrating Indians.

A few days later when all was forgotten and forgiven and life

once more became normal, Waraeki asked me to go with him
on a hunting expedition. A remarkable incident of this trip was
the shooting of a monkey by Waraeki, using an arrow poisoned
with curare. Taking no notice of us, a monkey family had been
playing noisily high up in the trees. There was ripe fruit everywhere and since humans can eat everything a monkey can and
these spoilt animals took only one bite at anything before throwing the rest away, we had a delicious meal from their left-overs.
It did not seem quite fair to me that after the meal Waraeki
aimed his poisoned arrow at a particularly fat monkey. After he
had been hit, the monkey continued to hold on to the branch
on which he had been swinging until the curare started to take
effect. Gradually his hands loosened and he dropped to the
ground dead. All this happened so quickly and noiselessly that
the other members of the family did not notice anything. This
was the first time I had seen the deadly curare arrow used. I
insisted on skinning and carving up the carcass, since the Cauaburys bake monkeys whole with fur and intestines. Waraeki
protested that I was spoiling a lovely meal, but he gave way
eventually and the monkey tasted wonderful, even when cooked
'à la European'.

After a two-day trek through the jungle we came to a palm-
leaf hut where we spent the night. Comfortably installed in our
hammocks, Waraeki and I talked until the early hours.

The hut in which we were staying had a special function in
the training of the young Cauaburys. Boys between fifteen and
seventeen years of age were brought here in groups by an 'Elder'
of the tribe for training. They live in this solitude for several
months on a strict diet of game, ants, the fruits of the jungle
and a drink made of corn-meal and water. The 'Elder', who is
the direct representative of the chief, initiates the boys in the
legends and traditions of the tribe, gives them an opportunity of
proving their skill as hunters and shows them how to learn the
tribes' complicated mask dances. They are also taught how to
play the drums and, most important, the Jurupari flute. This is
called 'The Demon Flute' and it plays an important part in the
beliefs and traditions of the natives. The entire tribe believes

that the flute has evil powers, especially against women, and a feast in its honour takes place every year.

After many months in the lonely jungle, the boys return to their villages where they are received with feasting and rejoicing. At this stage they are considered ready for marriage.

Waraeki told me of the simple marriage laws. A Cauabury Indian is never allowed to marry into his tribal group because it is considered that every member of his community is his brother or sister. The marriages of brothers and even cousins is in accordance with seniority. No fuss is made about getting married and no festivities or celebrations take place. The bride, who has often never seen the groom and whose parents have been presented with gifts previously, is abducted during the night by the bridegroom while the bride's family looks on in great amusement. The only thing the groom asks of his bride is that she works well and will bear him many children. Beauty does not make the slightest difference to him.

A week or so after my return to the village a drum began its strange throbbing from the mountain slopes; it continued day and night in a regular steady rhythm. Waraeki had become a different person. He hardly spoke to us and was obviously preoccupied with serious matters. I asked him what was wrong but he would only answer with a single word, 'Uakti', 'Uakti'. Eventually he explained secretively that 'Uakti' was the name of the old demon who would soon visit the tribe and play the magical Jurupari flute on the first moonless night. While he was telling me this he kept looking round to make sure no one overheard.

All the women in the village were busy brewing cashiri from the yuca fruit. Vast quantities of the stuff were fermenting in hollowed tree trunks, and there was no doubt that a great feast was in the offing.

Soon the two hundred and fifty people living in our village increased to three hundred. Next day I counted three hundred and forty. The next almost four hundred. I felt uncomfortable and wondered how the visitors would behave towards us and if they would lose their self-restraint under the influence of drink

The author (third from right) joining in Macu dance (see page 139)

Women are the pack-animals of the Indians

Tucano girl

Tucano men with blowpipes

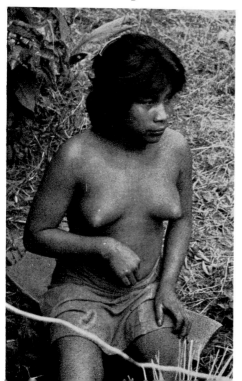

and the spell of the demon flute. I considered leaving but I also felt that if we stayed we would experience something quite sensational and of extraordinary human interest. I decided to stay and let the guardian angel look after us, as he had done many times before.

The deep monotonous beat of the drums continued. We awoke in the mornings bleary-eyed and apprehensive. Then one day we saw that the men, women and children were busy painting themselves with special care. A new pattern of long snake-like lines running from foot to forehead in red, blue or black appeared on the naked bodies of the natives. Graciela's doting playmates no longer came to our hut and the women with their babies did not visit Aenne. Before, they had come every morning to take my wife's hand and lay it on the forehead of their babies, believing that the magic of this white woman with her blonde hair would protect their children from disease. We noticed that the children looked at us aggressively and we felt that their parents were avoiding us. Tension mounted hour by hour during the day and we felt sure that this was to be the night when the magic Jurupari flute would be played.

In the evening I crept into the village which was now over-crowded with at least a thousand visitors squatting in groups around the fires talking in subdued but excited voices. Whenever they saw me I felt their suspicious stare, but for the time being we were still safe through Waraeki's protection. It worried me that I could never discover an actual chieftain who had the power to control these primitive peoples, although it was clear from the great number of male visitors that there must have been many villages represented here. I decided that probably the spiritual leaders, medicine-men and chieftains would arrive before the feast reached its climax. I wondered with mixed feelings of fear and curiosity if one of these would play the dreaded Jurupari flute in our village? The most maddening thing was not to be able to understand what was being said around us.

At last I found Waraeki who was preoccupied and did not want to remain with me. But I held him by his shoulders and begged him to explain. He must have felt the urgency of my request

I

since he asked me to follow him into a thicket where we talked in whispers. It seemed that every Cauabury village had a Jurupari flute which was hidden away in a different place every year. Any woman who was unfortunate enough to set eyes on it was immediately killed. It occurred to me that the scarcity of females in our village was a result of this cruel practice. And yet I also knew that any deficiency in the numbers of women was regularly replenished with girls kidnapped in raids on other villages. I could see that some of Graciela's playmates had far darker skins than others, but I had never seen the mothers of these children. Perhaps they were hidden from us? But Waraeki was not in a mood to answer these questions and he went away leaving me guessing.

I returned home to try and reassure my family. I was not very successful because the atmosphere was becoming increasingly strange and eerie. In the village the natives still sat talking round their fires and it seemed that no one had yet begun drinking.

Suddenly Waraeki stood inside our hut. His whole body, including his face, was painted in fantastic designs. We hardly recognised him and Graciela, who trusted and loved him, hid behind her mother. He had come to tell us that all the visiting hordes knew that we were honoured guests. He had told them that we had saved his life and that we were his friends. Still it would be better, he said, if we were not seen in the village that night. Graciela and Aenne must in no circumstances take the risk of seeing the Jurupari, as this would mean certain death.

It was a close, hot night and we felt more helpless and apprehensive; even the frogs and grasshoppers were silent. Only large glow-worms twinkled unceasingly through the darkness. They were so bright that I could recognise the outlines of our surroundings in their light.

Suddenly a shrill note pierced the night. Two others followed. There was a short pause and then came more staccato notes which grew faster and faster and shriller and shriller until they mixed in a whirl. We heard women scream and the crackle and rustle of branches and bushes as people ran in all directions. Graciela began to cry and we were unable to comfort her. I could not

stand the oppressive closeness of our hut and promising not to
be away long, ran towards the village.

Out of breath I stumbled and fell into some bushes just before
reaching the village. My heart was beating so violently that I
had to press my hand on it to relieve the pain. I trembled with
excitement and exhaustion while the close tropical heat of the
night seemed to suffocate me. A long chain of shadow-like figures
moved in the jungle, but passed without noticing me. A naked
foot trod on my hand, but I held my breath and did not dare
move. When the figures slowly shaped themselves into recognisable human beings, I could see that they were playing instruments and that they were moving in a slow dignified rhythm.
Some were producing the shrill sounds that had frightened us
earlier, playing a kind of wooden shepherd's flute, while others
produced monotonous deep sounds on a long, thick bamboo pipe.
I felt sure that neither could be the Jurupari. When these strange
figures had passed, I crept after them as they moved towards
the river.

In the darkness I tore my skin and the blood stuck to my
damp body. I collided with fire-ants and my body felt pierced by
a thousand red-hot needles. Then I stumbled into a bush of
thorny wild bamboo, overgrown by liana. My arms and legs
stuck in a maze of spiky branches and creepers and I was helplessly suspended above ground with my legs trying to gain a
firm hold somewhere.

'Take it easy, control yourself!' I kept on repeating. 'For
God's sake don't panic.' The close damp heat had taken my
breath away and I fainted. A disgustingly sweet smell brought
me to my senses again and I recognised the smell of some flowers
which at night exude a poisonous odour. Desperate fear overcame me, but at least it forced me out of my state of exhaustion
and I regained control over my limbs. I disentangled myself by
biting through the creepers. They left a nauseating bitter taste
in my mouth, my gums began to swell and my mouth was
like parchment.

The shrill music of the flutes had disappeared but suddenly
a dull, uncanny, groaning sound filled the air. There was nothing

earthly or real about this noise; I could only compare it with the last cry of a dying animal.

The Jurupari! This was the call of the Jurupari, the strange instrument which the demon Uakti, at the beginning of time, had taught the tribe to play.

Soon the Indians returned from the river bank led by the man who had collected the Jurupari from its hiding place. I crept back to the village and hid close to the large open space surrounded by huts where the procession halted among a great many fires. The scene was lit up clearly and I recognised a vigorous old man enticing notes from the Jurupari; sounds which sent a shiver down my spine. Everybody who heard it was under the influence of this strange instrument. A long row of men danced forwards and backwards with monotonous rhythms in front of the demon flute player. Each dancer rested a hand on the next man's shoulder and with his free hand produced a deep, hollow sound from his shepherd's flute, or swung a rattle in time with his steps. These strange sounds and rhythms were accompanied by a monotonous humming.

Swiftly the whole fantastic performance stopped, the strange notes were muted, and from the Jurupari came a long, suffering, wailing note. While this note was held, the row of dancing Indians formed into a circle around the old man. He broke their circle with one determined leap and as if in flight disappeared into the jungle to hide once more the Jurupari flute on the banks of the river.

The last note of the Jurupari was the signal for the women to return and one by one they came cautiously from their hiding places. From large bowls made of hollowed calabash fruits they offered the men the potent cashiri beer. After each man had emptied his bowl in one long draught, the *dabucuri* dance, the dance of the angry demon, started again, but this time because the flute was hidden, in the presence of the women. The men danced in a row, moving up and down the open space, stamping their right feet on the ground every time they reversed direction. At every turn a girl squeezed herself between two of the male dancers who dropped their left hands on to the girl's shoulder.

In this way the row of dancers weaved to and fro until a girl had squeezed herself between each of the men. Dancers and onlookers were united in their ecstasy. Even in my hideout I found it difficult to remain calm.

Then dramatically there was a woman's scream, growing shriller and more penetrating. Branches broke in my immediate vicinity and a body slumped against a tree which was leaning at an angle over my hiding-place. In the light of the fire I watched a desperate struggle take place a few feet from me.

I recognised the old man who had blown the Jurupari. He was dragging a wildly struggling girl towards the open space who was fighting with the desperation which only the fear of death can produce. As the strength of the medicine-man began to fade, he let out a scream. Immediately two husky young men disengaged themselves from the dancers, grabbed hold of the unfortunate girl and pushed her against a tree. The tree was rotten and crashed down from the impact, just missing me.

When I recovered from the shock I heard a general hubbub from the crowd. The dancing group had disintegrated and the women had fled in panic into the jungle. Now the girl, who had been dragged into the middle of the open space, was surrounded by a crowd of excitedly yelling men who pushed and jostled her into an empty hut. I waited with feverish excitement for what would happen next—wondering if the girl had seen the Jurupari while the medicine-man was hiding it again.

Everybody now tried to get into the medicine-man's hut, but the majority were left standing outside talking excitedly. As my hiding place was too far away for me to observe what was going on, I crept to the side of the hut. I took off my clothes and blackened my body with burnt pieces of wood which were lying around. Thus adorned, and with most of the Indians already drunk, I had a good chance of not being spotted. There was a continuous coming and going and dancers formed everywhere in groups.

A tortured scream pierced the night. I crawled close to the hut and spying through its palm-leaf walls I saw the medicine-man and the two young Indians who had captured the girl. She lay dead on the floor. This was too much for me and I thought I would lose my nerve. I quickly crawled back to where I had left my clothes in a thicket and lit a cigarette to steady my nerves.

When I returned to the open space, where the fires were still burning brightly, dawn was breaking. Some of the natives had started to build a funeral pyre and were dragging branches and logs from the jungle. Then the medicine-man came out of the hut, followed by the two young Indians carrying the body of the girl which was painted bright red from top to toe. Walking round the funeral pyre, the medicine-man drew magic signs in the air with a little stick and mumbled a spell. The two Indians placed the body of the girl on the bonfire and lit it with a torch of reeds. As the flames burst out, the medicine-man scratched signs of circles and snakes on the ground.

The flames rose angrily from the dry wood, and with a crackling and hissing sound, shot high into the greying sky, enveloping the body.

Hundreds of drunk Indians were now dancing round the fire in a cloud of dust, singing a monotonous song. The women emerged again from their hiding places and once more handed the men bowls of cashiri.

The fire was still burning at daybreak. The Indians were now so drunk that they did not notice me in my black nakedness. Soon a rain shower extinguished the fire. The medicine-man pulled out the charred body and handed it to the two young Indians. They carried the corpse to a hollow tree trunk where they broke the bones and threw the pieces into the trunk. The tree was obviously an ancient relic which for generations had been used for this gruesome purpose. Then they began to grind down the bones with heavy wooden clubs and it looked as if this would continue for many hours. Only then did I remember my wife and child, and decided it was high time to get back to them.

Not recognising me in my 'war-paint', Graciela screamed when I entered the hut. Aenne was worried and entreated me to leave at once. Before we could discuss the details, Waraeki came reeling into the hut—very drunk. In words which were even more difficult to understand than usual, he confirmed that it would be better for us to disappear for a time, and wait for him a two days' trip away on a sandbank. When the feast was over he would come and fetch us. He told us that the demon flute had been seen during the night by a girl and she had been sacrificed. All the men were in a high state of excitement and he could not guarantee our safety any longer. Threats against us had already been voiced, especially by a man whose brother had been killed by a white man during a raid. I decided to leave immediately and told Waraeki that we would return after the second rainy season. Waraeki left us but I don't think he realised in his drunkenness that this was our farewell. Still I hoped that he would remember my promise to return after the second rainy season. I was determined to take some photographs and make a film of the life of the Cauabury tribe.

Aenne was very nervous and in a great hurry to leave. Graciela, too, was anxious. I found it difficult to persuade them that there was no danger during the day as the natives were drunk. They would only come to fetch us, if at all, at night. The best time to escape would be in the hot afternoon, when the Cauaburys would be worn out from drinking and dancing and would fall asleep. Before we left I simply had to find out what would happen to the ground flesh and bones of the girl. So, in spite of the protests of my family, I returned, still black and naked, to the festivities.

The medicine-man and his two helpers had left the tree trunk and other Indians had taken over the job of pulverising the girl's remains. When the medicine-man reappeared, he was in the company of several Indians whose naked bodies were adorned with coloured ara feathers. They were greeted with great respect and ceremony by the Indians who were grinding the bones.

With a wave of his hand the medicine-man signified that the work should stop. Slowly he let the fine dust run through his fingers. Then he took a bowl filled with red fruit and with a small rounded piece of wood he mashed them into pulp; to this he added the dust, stirring all the time.

The medicine-man, very seriously and with measured movements, performed these rites to the accompaniment of a monotonous chanting from the onlookers. In the meantine the girl's remains had been mixed with the fruit pulp into a sticky, red substance. The medicine-man dipped his finger into it and painted designs on the faces and bodies of his helpers. This ceremony took place in tense silence. At the end of it, using the remnants of the red mixture, one of the helpers painted signs of lightning and snakes on the body and face of the medicine-man.

The major part of the bone powder still remained in the hollowed-out tree. Now the medicine-man poured some of the strongly fermented cashiri juice into the tree where he mixed it carefully with what was left of the girl. The women had disappeared again as the demon Uakti would not tolerate their presence during these most holy of all rites. When the tree was practically filled with cashiri, and well mixed with the remains of the girl, the medicine-man ceremoniously and in one draught, drank a small bowl of it. Then he handed it to his helpers and then to the other Indians who drank until there was nothing left in the tree trunk.

The medicine-man, accompanied by the warriors, returned to the hut where the girl had been clubbed to death. I followed them, and through an opening at the back of the hut watched them preparing a ritual dance. The faces and bodies of the dancers were painted in a glowing red, and as they moved forward and backward to the beat of the drums the feathers of their tall headgear whipped through the air. Although there was bright sunshine outside, it was gloomily dark within. I felt disappointed not to be able to photograph this evil scene, but I could not risk drawing attention to my presence by using flash-light.

When the official ceremony was over the feast really started. The women returned from their hiding places once more and the drinking began in earnest. An Indian feast of this nature usually lasts for many days and nights until every drop of the vast quantities of drink have been finished.

The crowds in the open space in front of the huts had thinned out, but in the nearby woods pairs and groups of Indians were making love, oblivious of their surroundings. Most of them were very drunk, but there was no fighting and the effects of the cashiri seemed to encourage universal love and carefree drowsiness.

I felt the moment had come when we could leave this strange place unnoticed. Once these most primitive of all primitives awoke from their drunkenness, there might be no further opportunity of slipping away safely.

Aenne and Graciela were very happy to see me back again as they were still frightened.

The moist brooding jungle heat was now at its worst, vibrating the air over every open space. The few Indians who were still about had sunk to the ground in a deep drunken sleep as we dragged our things to the river. Exhausted and trembling with the nervous strain of the last forty-eight hours we climbed into Waraeki's dugout and escaped from the spell of the demon flute.

10

Missionaries

AFTER an uneventful trip down the river Cauabury, in Waraeki's dugout, we changed into the motor-boat which took us safely to São Gabriel. As the first terrifying rapids of the Rio Negro begin just above the town, we decided to rest for a few days, to restock our provisions and decide upon our future plans.

São Gabriel is the seat of the Bishop of the Salesiana Mission. The Bishop we met was José Domotrovitch, a kind and helpful man who had come to the territory about forty years ago as Padre José and had made it his life's work to convert the Indians of north-west Brazil to Christianity. One should really say reconvert, because missionaries had worked in this territory a hundred years before. But they had remained for only a few decades and after their departure the 'converts' soon returned to their earlier beliefs. All that survived were a few festivals such as São Pedro, São Pablo and São Juan, which were celebrated by the Indians with enthusiasm and with liberal quantities of alcohol.

During the last thirty years much of the lost ground has been reclaimed, not so much by the priests but by the fanatical European Sisters of the mission. I remember with horror watching the native girls, who are by nature so gay and friendly, leaving church after early Mass, in single file, and with now downcast eyes. Silently, under the strict supervision of one of the Sisters, they were marched back to their spartan quarters to live their narrow lives divorced from the beauty of their surroundings. These children of nature who should have been laughing, playing, flirting and enjoying their country now spent

their time mumbling prayers and fingering their rosaries.
It was soon obvious to us that the Sisters of the mission at
Sao Gabriel were a lot less popular than the priests. With few
exceptions, their talents for winning the Indians' hearts and
converting their souls were strictly limited. The Bishop, who was
obviously aware of these shortcomings, seemed powerless to
repair them. Although he had ordered that food should be
brought to our rooms, it did not arrive. When I asked the reason
for this, I was told by the Mother Superior, who looked at me
with contempt and suspicion, that she could not possibly send
one of her Indian girls across the road to waste time on the way
talking to Indian men. Her expression and the tone of her voice
as she emphasised the words 'Indian' and 'men' showed her
hatred of anything masculine. Eventually she arranged for an
Indian boy to bring us our food.

The Sisters were frightened that the eyes of a man might
awake the romantic feelings of their girl charges, and as the
opportunities were greatest in church, the girls were strictly
forbidden to let their eyes stray from their folded hands. It
seemed to us that the Bishop's orders were regularly sabotaged
by the Sisters. Many of the priests shook their heads disapprov-
ingly, and agreed with us that the holy Sisters should pray a
little less and live a little more.

I am glad to say that such conditions did not prevail everywhere.
At the missionary station of Yavarete, which we visited later, there
was an entirely different atmosphere. There the Mother Superior
was an open-hearted young Brazilian woman who had the special
gift of being able to win the hearts of the natives who adored her.

The Bishop invited us to spend the Christmas of 1954 in
Yavarete. This promised to be interesting as every year over two
thousand Indians, with their families, arrived at the settlement
to celebrate the festival. All these people camped in the surroundings and were fed by the missionaries.

So we set off, led by an Indian pilot, and hoped to reach
Yavarete which lies on the Rio Uaupes at the borders of Colombia
and Brazil before the holiday began. Due to the many rapids our
progress was slow at first, and had it not been for the amazing

skill of the pilot, we would never have succeeded in getting our heavily-laden craft up this part of the river.

The Rio Uaupes is a peaceful river and we chugged along happily. There were huge sandbanks on either side of the black water, dazzling white against the deep green of the thick jungle, and the dawns and sunsets were as unusual and beautiful as any we had seen. From time to time we passed picturesque Indian huts decked with palm-leaves. Our only disappointment was the natives who were often dressed in a variety of ill-assorted town garments given them by the missionaries. Most of the Indians in this region belonged to the Tucano tribe and had seasonal homes by the river. During the dry season they collect turtle eggs, catch and smoke the fish which live in abundance in the warm waters of the river, and fatten themselves for the lean season when the rains come. They collect rubber and Brazil nuts, and the yellow fruits of the pupunha palm. This fruit is cooked to taste like potatoes or made into an alcoholic brew of considerable potency. The natives use the fibres of the tucuma palm-tree to make beautiful hammocks which they carry with them wherever they go, and also make beautifully carved stools and artistic baskets. The men hunt with blowpipes, the arrows of which are dipped in curare. A leaf from one of the plants used for this poison when dissolved in a little water can paralyse the tongue for several hours and the men, it is said, use it frequently when annoyed by a nagging wife.

Our Indian pilot had friends and relatives all along our route, so we spent many nights with the natives in their huts. The second night after our departure from São Gabriel we stayed in the hut of the pilot's brother-in-law while a thunderstorm raged outside. Aenne and Graciela caused a lot of amusement among the native women when they tried to cook the beans presented to us by the Bishop. However much they cooked and stirred them, they simply would not get soft. One of the women offered something to my wife. She was just going to put it into her mouth when Graciela said 'Mummy, always look first before you eat.' We all looked carefully in the dim light, and to our amazement we saw a crawling ball of locusts in Aenne's hand. To these natives, locusts are a delicacy. They tear the heads off the insects and swallow their fat little bodies with loud appreciative munching sounds. My wife and Graciela could not be tempted, but I sampled these insects later and found the flavour interesting. I am sure one could develop a liking for them in time. Quite a few white people in these regions do, in fact, eat them.

We reached the village of Tatacusa, but unfortunately that was as far as we were able to travel and we spent Christmas at the missionary post there. At least a thousand Indian guests had arrived at the village for a great celebration, but it was impossible to persuade any of them to pilot our boat to Yavarete two days before Christmas Eve.

On Christmas Eve the beautifully decorated church overflowed with bare-footed Indians from the surrounding jungle. We could not take Graciela to the service which lasted from midnight to four in the morning, but the Sisters were thoughtful enough to send us candles, cakes and sweets so that we could arrange our own simple Christmas celebrations. In spite of all Graciela's letters to Father Christmas he had not managed to bring the sewing machine she had wished for, but a doll's cradle beautifully carved by the Tucano Indians was an adequate substitute. On Christmas Day we watched a play and listened to the children's recital in the girls' school and I was persuaded to give a mouth-organ concert. There was quite a happy Christmas atmosphere and the discipline was less severe than in São Gabriel. Here I would say, the native children had plenty of fun and appeared to live a fairly natural life.

We continued our journey on Boxing Day, accompanied by some Indian families making for home. We towed six of their canoes until we came to the great waterfalls of Ipanore where we left our motor-boat with a local family. Now we set out on foot to a lonely place in the jungle above the waterfalls where we had to wait for a week for a *lancha* to Yavarete. Early in the New Year the *lancha* arrived and within thirty-six hours we were in Yavarete.

The settlement had been warned of our impending visit and when we came into view a little Indian girl ran to the German nun with the news that the nun's brother and sister had arrived. The Sister could not understand what the little Indian meant until it was explained that visitors were coming who had golden hair and who must therefore be relatives.

A German priest also lived at the settlement and one of his jobs was to look after the meteorological station. He went to Yavarete before the first world war as the valet of an aristocrat on a safari, but had been left behind because of a serious attack of malaria. He swore that if he recovered he would become a missionary and never return to his homeland.

Everybody was kind and friendly to us and, in return for the hospitality we received, I photographed an airfield which the mission had undertaken to build with the help of local Indian labour and primitive equipment. During our stay the director of the mission offered us two Indian guides and provisions for a week's trip to the Sierra de los Puercos—'The Pigs' Heights'—to visit another Indian tribe.

Using a canoe, and led by the two Indians, we travelled up the Rio Tapura, which flows into the Rio Uaupes just below Yavarete, and spent the first night with a Macu family. The Macus are considered the lowest form of human life by many Indians and are, at times, treated rather like animals. When a Macu is given clothing by the missionaries, it is soon taken from him by members of other tribes who reason that animals do not need clothing. Most Macus wear nothing but a G-string.

The Macus are often used as forced labour by other tribes and are frequently kept as slaves. They are an honest, hard-working and modest people but their chief talents lie in the preparation of a specially deadly curare poison.

In olden days, one legend says, the Macu Indians lived on the banks of the Rio Negro, but were driven to small rivulets in the interior by invading warrior tribes. When the Macus had eaten all the fish in the small rivers, a famine overtook them and they feared they would die of hunger. But a good demon appeared to their *tuchaua*—their chief—and said he would show them how to live in the woods without fish. The demon took him into the woods and using a long bamboo pipe, blew a small arrow at a

large animal which collapsed and died. The *tuchaua* stared at
the demon with amazement, not understanding how such a small
arrow could kill such a large animal.

The demon then showed the *tuchaua* how to make a blowpipe
and also led him to the five different plants which contained the
poison for the arrow. Since that time the Macus have lived in the
centre of the jungle jealously guarding the secret of the poison.
Even today they are still the masters in the preparation of
poisons and Indians from many tribes visit them to trade for
their famous poisons.

The Macu Indians are only happy in the woods. They are
small and backward compared with the other Indians of the
region. They live from hunting and fishing and on the fruits of
the jungle. Insects are also part of their diet and they regularly
eat ants, beetles, worms and snails. The Macus especially love
caimans, a kind of alligator, and several species of snakes, and
they are wonderful shots with blowpipes and bows and arrows.

They usually live in large *malocas*—communal huts—which
often house as many as eighty people. From time to time quarrels
break out between the generations and when the younger
generation becomes dissatisfied with the old chief or medicine-
man, they leave and build themselves new *malocas* in a different
area. The Macus stay away from their homes for many months
at a time roaming the jungle for game. Keeping on the move,
they go from one hunting ground to the other, staying at each
until the game has been hunted and the fish caught. During
these travels each family stays together, building provisional huts
and clearing patches of forest to plant maize and mandioca. The
virgin soil is so rich that it will bear three crops a year, but the
Macus can hardly be called agriculturists. As soon as they leave
after the harvest their small plantations are swallowed up by the
jungle. At the end of their wanderings the groups meet again and
live together in their communal huts for several months.

The further we paddled the narrower the Rio Tapura became.
Giant trees lay across it from one bank to the other and we had
to use axes and jungle knives to cut through them. On the third
day I decided it was hopeless to continue by boat and sent one of

our two Indians back to Yavarete with the canoe. I got four Macu Indians to help carry our luggage and we set out on foot to reach the Sierra de los Puercos, where we hoped to find a large *maloca*.

There was hardly a track through the thick jungle, and we had a difficult time trying to keep up with the tough Macu Indians, although they were carrying our heavy luggage and ten-foot-long blowpipes. Exhausted we reached the *maloca* during the late afternoon.

When we were within a hundred yards of the *maloca*, the bearers halted and asked me to lead them as custom prescribed. So as not to alarm the settlement by our sudden appearance, I clapped my hands and yodelled with great gusto as I led the way. When we reached the *maloca* I found terrified old women and children cowering in the corners. As soon as the bearers spoke to them in their own language they recovered a little but still watched us suspiciously. Soon the men began to return from their hunting and fishing expeditions and the young women also came back carrying large baskets of wild fruits, bananas and mandioca from their plantations.

All the food was handed to the *tuchaua*, the chief of the *maloca*. He passed everything to several women who immediately began preparing a meal over an open fire. No one took any notice of us, so I hung up our hammocks in the least crowded part of the communal hut.

There were at least ten different fires burning in the hut and around every fire squatted a family roasting corn cobs, bananas or game. A main dish was being prepared in two huge pots over the larger fires and at another fire, girls were roasting large mandioca pancakes. When the first pancake was ready, an old woman offered us a piece. It tasted remarkably good. When we had finished it another woman brought us a calabash filled with a cold brew made of mandioca flour and water. Now that we were sharing their meal, we could consider ourselves guests of the tribe. The chief, who had been talking for a long time with our bearers, came over to greet us by letting us touch the tips of his fingers, a form of greeting which was probably the result of contact with the mission.

Indian woman feeding birds

Rapids, Rio Caroni, Venezuela

Entrance to underground Waika hut (see page 156)

Above: *the author dressed as a chief at the Macu feast (see page* 139)

Right: *Waika girl (see page* 155)

Medicine-man blowing illness away

Medicine-man sucking out illness

I presented the chief with a large piece of tobacco. His eyes
lit up as he disappeared with it, followed by a crowd of children
clamouring 'just a tiny bit' as children at home ask for sweets.
The ice had been broken and other members of the tribe came
to touch fingertips. Even the women came without fear, and
Aenne gave a small present to everyone who greeted us. Tobacco
was by far the most popular of our gifts but such things as sewing
needles, a reel of thread, fishing hooks, were also appreciated.

Night approached and sixty-eight hammocks were fixed in a
fairly unplanned sort of way all round the large hut. Often two
Indians, especially children, shared the same hammock. Just
before going to sleep a broth made of boiled leaves and roots
mixed with mandioca flour was prepared. The *tuchaua* personally
handed the soup and mandioca pancakes to every family. It
seemed that a sort of primitive communism regulated life in the
camp. Everybody had to work for the community and its head
distributed the fruits of this labour to each. If one or the other
family was dissatisfied, they were free to move out.

There were no mosquitos or vermin to pester us and we were
able to rest comfortably in our hammocks and listen to the
conversations of the families. The guide and interpreter who
had been assigned to me by the mission, hung his hammock near
mine so that I was able to ask him what was being said. Food,
hunting and other Macu tribes were their main subjects of conversation, I was told.

So we dozed and relaxed, satisfied with life amongst people
who had no idea that there was such a thing as the sea, or a city
called London or an invention called the atom bomb. They knew
only that other tribes lived in the jungle and were either peace-
loving or war-like, and of good and bad demons. Yet I am sure
that these primitive peoples got more satisfaction out of life than
the average civilised person.

The Indians hung their hammocks as near as possible to the
fires and slept naked except for a G-string. It became chilly during
the night and they shivered when the cold air touched them.
Then the men would make animal-like grunting sounds and the
women would have to get up and put logs on the fires. When a

K

woman was angry or dissatisfied with her man she would put a lot of wood on the fire and watch gleefully as the flames touched his naked buttock and shot him out of his hammock, cursing and swearing.

When the sun rose, the men remained in their hammocks talking idly and laughing, while the women got up to feed their babies and make up the fires. Only after the men had drunk cold mandioca soup, eaten a roasted banana and some corn-on-the-cob, did they get out of their hammocks. Later they went fishing or hunting, or joined the women gathering fruit, leaving the old women and children behind in the *maloca*.

The young Indians grow up without any guidance and are left entirely to their own devices. It seemed to me that they learned to walk and talk earlier than our children. The girls are given responsibility at an early age and five-year-olds help with the housework and look after their younger brothers and sisters. At that age, in fact, they start a life of endless toil. In contrast, the boys have a wonderful time. By the time they are eight they have almost complete freedom and go fishing and hunting. The jungle becomes their playground.

When the old people reach the age when they can no longer work, they face a time of desperation and suffering. No Macu has any use for old people. They are never called mother or father, only contemptuously 'the old man' or 'the old woman'. When they are ill they are left in their hammocks in a space far from the fire. If a sick old person does not get better, the medicine-man tells the relatives that the body is poisoned. At this point the whole settlement takes an interest in the affair and all the tribe squats around the invalid, not because they feel sorry for him, but simply to watch the spectacle of death. They whisper such remarks as: 'He'll be dead by the time the sun sets' or 'There is only a little life left in him' or 'Look, his breathing is very uneven now'.

As soon as the victim is dead, everyone begins to cry as custom demands. A rough sort of coffin is hastily knocked together and once the person has been buried in a shallow grave his name is never mentioned again.

The Macus and many other Indian tribes believe that all diseases originate from poisons. They also think that white people and foreigners wander through the land spreading poison in the shape of influenza. The Indians had not experienced this until the white people arrived in the jungle, so they have no resistance to it. An attack of 'flu often kills a native, and they are terrified of it.

An incident that happened not long ago illustrates the Indian's attitude. A Colombian trader wanted some packing-cases carried through the jungle to by-pass some rapids. The natives refused to carry them because they had been told by other traders that the boxes contained 'flu poison. The Colombian knew this was a shabby trick played on him by his rivals, but his explanations were not accepted by the frightened Indians. Even when the trader offered to treble the wages he could find no one willing to help him. In desperation he told the *tuchaua* of the local tribe that if he did not order his men to do as he asked, he would open the boxes and spread the 'flu poison over the whole village. Terror-stricken the *tuchaua* consulted his subjects who instantly, and without demanding any pay, shifted the packing cases.

There is no leprosy or syphilis, otherwise so common in South America, among the Macus, but dysentery is very common. If a Macu is sick he stays in his hammock until the medicine-man gives him herbs and concoctions which are administered to the accompaniment of mumblings of formulae supposed to drive the poison out of the body. If this does not help, the medicine-man relies on magical hocus-pocus and on tobacco smoke which is supposed to drive away evil spirits. It is a sad day for the patient when the medicine-man decides to give up, as no one else will do anything for him from then on. Relatives begin to cry and start to prepare his coffin before his eyes. The coffin is usually the dead man's canoe, cut in half and bound together with the body inside. If the dead man does not possess a canoe, the body is wrapped in his hammock and buried. In their hurry to get rid of the body, it has been known for the hammock to be sewn up while the sick person was still alive. If an abnormal child is born it is buried alive by its parents who believe that anyway it would not survive. When twins are born, one of them is destroyed as the Macus think that a mother does not have enough milk for two children. Yet I have seen a puppy, and even a jaguar cub, sucking a woman's breast while she fed her own child with the other.

Although the Macus bathe several times a day, they never seem clean. Nor do they worry about looking dirty. Most primitive Indians clean the running nose of a child by sucking it. When a priest explained that this was not very nice, he was told that it was much better than his habit of collecting the dirt and carrying it about in a piece of cloth. Indian logic is sometimes hard to contradict.

The women returned at midday on the first day of our stay at the Macu camp. On their backs they carried heavy baskets filled with mandioca roots. These little roots, looking like small carrots except that they are brown in colour, were immediately grated on a piece of wood studded with little stones. The result was a messy substance like grated potatoes. The juice of this stuff is poisonous and had to be removed. This was done by stuffing the mash into a raffia bag which was hung up and squeezed by turning a stick fixed through a loop at the bottom of the bag. The pressed-out juice was collected in a container and the dry substance left in the bag—called farinha or mandioca flour—tipped on a large clay-plate over the fire and roasted into pancakes. The women also made many kinds of drinks from this flour, often merely mixing it with water and heating it into a soup.

After a large amount of mandioca pancakes had been baked, the women cut them up and threw the pieces into a hollowed-out tree trunk where they were mixed with water. When our interpreter saw me looking at this uninviting brew, he told me that a kashiri feast was being prepared in my honour. To speed up the process of fermentation the women fished out pieces of pancake from the fire, chewed them vigorously, then spat them back into the brew. Other women fed sugar-cane through a wooden press to add juice to the brew. Later all sorts of leaves and roots were added. Finally a fire was built next to the hollow tree trunk and this was kept alight all night so that the gentle warmth would hasten the fermentation.

Indian at Orinoco mission

Macu slave-boy

Macu slave-girl

During the two days it took the kashiri to mature, everyone was enthusiastically busy with the preparation for the feast. A tapir and several monkeys were shot and the meat smoked; I handed out round after round of tobacco to add to the good cheer and to cement my friendship with the Macus. After two days and nights of fermentation the liquid from the tree trunk was poured through a large strainer and the drinking started immediately. The men painted themselves and me, and we decorated ourselves with coloured feathers. Then the dancing commenced.

I think I must have been the first white man ever to join in a Macu dance and I quickly became the centre of attraction. With hands on each others shoulders we formed into a monotonously-swaying chain to the beat of hide drums. After the first dance the *tuchaua* ceremoniously handed me a stomach girdle made of the pointed teeth of jaguars. We continued dancing and the young girls who had until now only watched us, giggling and whispering comments about the men to each other, joined in the fun and squeezed themselves between the dancing men. So it went on, hour after hour, in simple steps, while we swayed forward and backwards with bodies touching only intermittently. Occasionally the dancing stopped long enough for the dancers to empty a bowl filled with kashiri, offered by one of the women. By lunchtime everybody was drunk and I succeeded in disengaging myself long enough to take some photographs.

Next morning, everyone was still dazed and I had some difficulty in persuading the bearers and our interpreter to get ready to leave. I wanted to cross the Sierra de los Puercos as far as the Rio Papuri and to return from there by canoe to Yavarete.

It was some time before I could organise my willing, but still tipsy Indian companions for the journey, but at last we were ready. With two extra Macus to carry the loot I had collected, our party was nine strong. We set out in a swaying, disorderly but happily singing caravan, loaded with blowpipes, poisoned arrows, carved stools and gaily-decorated baskets.

Four days later we returned safely to the respectability of the mission station at Yavarete.

11

Across the Casiquiare

AFTER a few days at the mission station at Yavarete we returned to the place above the rapids where we had left the motor-boat in the care of a Tucano Indian. I had asked him to take it out of the water and to stop up the cracks with plant fibres and tar. We were delighted to find that he had done the job well, and for the first time we had a watertight craft.

We were now ready to tackle the famous Casiquiare watershed which connects the vast river systems of the Amazon and Orinoco and which is supposed to run from the Orinoco to the Amazon in the wet season, and from the Amazon to the Orinoco in the dry season.

Our collection of trophies had increased considerably and we had great difficulty in finding room for them in the already overloaded boat. I loaded and unloaded several times, but there was always something left over. Then I repeated my last mistake and stacked what was left on the roof. We had been going for barely ten minutes when the boat almost turned over and I had to make an emergency landing. There was nothing to do but leave behind some of the beautiful things we had collected and I had to face the fact that nothing more could be taken on board until at least a fortnight's supply of petrol had been consumed. We had thirty five-gallon cans on board and could not count on obtaining more until we reached the middle of the Orinoco.

The Rio Negro was no longer broad and terrifying and we could chug along without fear of sudden tropical storms. The first village we reached was São Felipe where they build the *lanchas* which navigate rather spasmodically the river system of the Rio Negro above the rapids and the Rio Uaupes. Just above São Felipe at the mouth of the Rio Icana, we bought some beautiful coloured basket work. They had gay patterns of red, blue-black and yellow in locally produced dyes. The genipa fruit gives the blue-black colour and the carayura the dark red. The fruits of this plant are dried and then dissolved in water in earthenware pitchers. After three days a red sediment falls to the bottom which then has to be washed several times in clear water. When the sediment has been dried and ground into a fine powder, it is kept in small calabash bowls until it is needed. The medicine-men believe that this carayura plant (bignonia chica) has tremendous magical powers of protection from evil spirits and great powers of healing wounds and disease.

The Indians who live in the thick jungle of this territory are mostly Tarianas, also called Tarias. Originally they came from the upper Orinoco in Venezuela. Their language is still very much like that of the Banivas. They insist that they are the sole descendants of Capiriculi, the son of the great Indian god. These Tarianas are known and feared as brave warriors and have driven many tribes out of their ancestral lands during their many migrations. One of the most outstanding of their characteristics is their humorous and positive attitude towards life. They always have something to laugh about, even in the most unpleasant situations. They are not very brainy people and cannot master elementary numerical problems, but they excel at handicrafts. Like the Macus, they live in large communal huts.

They believe, as do most primitive Indians, that the white people are great magicians in certain matters, but they never forget that there are things which no white man is able to do or understand. As long as they are left to live their own lives they keep their pride and self-confidence without becoming subservient.

The Tarianas behave with brotherly love and generosity within the tribe, but they have no warmth or sympathy towards strangers, white or Indian. Things outside their tribe and immediate surroundings do not interest them.

As with all the tribes we visited, the Tarianas have a touching love towards their children and grandchildren. But as soon as children grow up they forget their parents and lose all feeling for them.

We travelled due north through wild jungle landscape, spending the nights in our hammocks on the banks of the Rio Negro. We never had any difficulty in finding food for the water was full of fish and there was plenty of wild fruit. We were now east of the Rio Cauabury, the territory of the Cauabury Indians. This is still a land full of mystery and barely explored. We wondered how many Indian tribes still roamed the jungle knowing nothing of civilisation, and still living as they did hundreds of years ago. We could not spare the time for another adventure to find out, as we now had travelled for almost four years and had a long way to go before reaching the open sea.

It seemed incongruous and unreal when we came to the little Brazilian border-post of Cucuhy, where uniformed customs officials inspected and stamped our passports. They were very friendly and welcomed the opportunity of talking to strangers. Their only contact with the outside world was a monthly aeroplane which brought food and mail. Unfortunately they could not give us any information on the chances of navigating the remainder of the Rio Negro and the Casiquiare. All they could tell us was that once we got to the Orinoco our lives would be made unbearable by swarms of mosquitos. As an appropriate farewell present the commandant gave us two bottles of mosquito oil.

Once past the Brazilian border-station we came across an enormous rock shaped like a sugar-loaf. Without warning it rises inexplicably over six hundred feet out of the endless flat jungle on the left bank of the Rio Negro. It marks the frontiers of Venezuela and Brazil, like a giant boundary-stone.

The guards at the Venezuelan border-post of Santa Rosa were also friendly but they were more inquisitive than the Brazilians. Customs officials tunnelled like ferrets through our luggage. When they found our Indian dancing masks all officious inspections were forgotten and they danced like madmen around our belongings. This suited us well. They had their fun and we became their friends. That evening we were asked to dinner with the telegraphist and his wife. I gave a mouth-organ concert, and an old gramophone sent its screechy tunes into the jungle until morning came.

After only two hours' sleep we pushed on. Colombia was now on one side of the river and Venezuela, the country which had been the starting point of our wanderings, on the other. It took us another two days to reach San Carlos, the southern capital of the Venezuelan State of Amazon.

Immediately behind San Carlos flows the Casiquiare which connects the Orinoco with the Rio Negro. There are formidable rapids at the confluence and both rivers carry deep black waters. There are no signs of human habitation in the entire area. I can't remember how long it took us to get through these rapids, but it was a wearing and tricky manoeuvre which finally left us with no idea of where we were and of what was going to come next. Finally we spotted the lonely figure of a woman, washing fruit by the river. She spoke Spanish and we learned with astonishment that we were already navigating the Casiquiare. I had wrongly assumed that the Casiquiare was a small canal of gently flowing waters. In fact it consists of one rapid after another. The rapids showed that the Casiquiare does *not* flow in different directions every six months as I had been assured by so many people. The Orinoco must be considerably higher than the Rio Negro, and the watershed can only flow one way the whole year round.

Although it was not the pleasant peaceful trip we had originally expected, and we had to battle with some of the most hellish rapids of our trip, part of our route led us through untouched loveliness. Smooth white sandbanks rose from the beautifully clear black water against the background of unpenetrable dark, green jungle. The further we went the more profuse and lush became the plant and animal life. No fishermen or game hunters bothered to penetrate the jungle further than a day's journey from San Carlos, so the area was entirely undisturbed and there were not even any mosquitos to plague us. Only later when the light-green waters of the Orinoco predominated did they descend on us in their swarms.

Two days later we spotted two dugouts struggling upstream. The natives were delighted when we took them in tow, in spite of the fact that we were making only slow progress. Four hours later when we reached a rapid which proved impossible to overcome with our boat, it was our turn to be pleased. The Indians, without us having to urge them on, helped us to empty our boat and carry our things across. After the freight came the empty boat. Slowly, yard by yard, for a whole afternoon, we pushed and lifted, and eventually managed to get across without damage.

From here onwards the Casiquiare became gentle and lethargic and gave us no surprises. It also became much wider at the place where the black waters of the Rio Siapa flowed in. The Rio Siapa is unexplored and as big as the Casiquiare and if it hadn't been for my map I would have inadvertently sailed up it. The scenery was still like paradise and there were hundreds of turtles. A few minutes every morning on a sandbank was long enough for us to collect a meal of turtle eggs. Where there are turtle eggs there are also wild beasts and snakes. Once we discovered jaguar tracks and it must have been an enormous animal which had prowled around our hammocks during the night.

After another few days of peaceful travelling through this wonderful luxuriant landscape we saw smoke rising. We were longing for information about our route, but by the time only a hundred yards divided us from the smoke it had become dark. The current was fast and turbulent and a suspicious rushing and splashing rose from the water; we had steered into the middle of a rapid and were engulfed in darkness. All I could do was to steer towards the few lights which now appeared. Suddenly, with a penetrating grinding noise, the boat heeled over and the screams of the three of us pierced the night. I jumped into the water, found I could touch ground, and supported the boat with my shoulder, my head only just above the water. We had hit a rock. In the light of a fire I could see people moving about not very far from us and I shouted for help. After a while two dugouts arrived and the natives assisted me to free the boat.

It was lucky that we tied up here because some way up river there was another dangerous place called *el paso del Diablo*—the devil's path. The Indians told us that we would never navigate it, so I took one of them along as pilot. Next morning, only a few hours after we started, we soon found ourselves in a labyrinth of rocks and boulders. Anyone not thoroughly familiar with the navigable canal, which wormed itself from one side of the river to the other, would have been hopelessly lost. This *paso del Diablo* was by far the worst, but also the last of the Casiquiare rapids and I could never have found my way through it alone. But it was no trouble with our pilot who knew every stone, above or below the water.

We paid the pilot in fish hooks, needles and tobacco and continued towards Capibara, a settlement which is the half-way mark on the Casiquiare between the Orinoco and the Rio Negro. We reached this place the next day and tied up close to the few houses. The settlement had a school-teacher, a Venezuelan whom the Government paid especially well to compensate for the loneliness of his job teaching the Indians how to read and write. We were lucky as the teacher had just returned from a small hunting expedition and the entire community was standing round a fire watching with rapture and anticipation the smoking of some succulent-looking boar's hams. We were immediately invited to join the party and the meat tasted as good as anything we have had since. The teacher gave us some encouraging news when he confirmed that we had passed all the important rapids of the Casiquiare.

From Capibara on it was again easy going. The river banks now often consisted of morasses, the colour of the water grew increasingly lighter, and thousands of tiny mosquitos descended on us and our hands, arms and face became swollen from the many stings. We tried the anti-mosquito liquid that the Brazilian commandant had given us and it helped a little and gave us something with which to defend ourselves.

From Capibara to the Orinoco we did not meet a soul. One afternoon we had difficulty in finding a place to tie up for the night. One bank of the river rose steeply, overgrown with impenetrable jungle, and on the other side was a morass. We searched for a place for hours and the sun was sinking when we saw the glittering reflection of a huge rock jutting out of the water. Just before it got dark our keel pushed against the rock and I jumped out to find something to which to fasten the boat. Graciela stood at the bow pouring out a continuous stream of good advice and sharp criticism. Suddenly she was silent, which made me stop and look at her. She tried to move her mouth, but no sound came out until she squeaked, 'Papi, look out! A huge snake. Here is your bush-knife.' I could hardly believe my eyes when I saw a huge anaconda on the rock a few feet away. It was coiled up and from the many knots in its body I guessed that it had eaten several animals and was now enjoying its digestive sleep. I approached the snake carefully, in my right hand the jungle knife and in my left the old shot gun which Aenne had handed to me. The anaconda must have noticed something, for it began moving leisurely as if it did not know what fear was. Aenne and Graciela stood petrified in the bow of the motor-boat looking at me and the anaconda in breathless tension. I remembered that I had not fastened the boat and I imagined myself already left alone on the rock with the monster.

I had to act quickly before the snake realised what was going on. I approached it slowly and I still remember the dazed stare with which it faced me while I lifted my arm and struck with all my might. The knife penetrated the tough hide, deep into the flesh and remained embedded in the spine. Within a second, movement electrified its whole body, although the knife in its back obstructed its freedom of movement considerably. But there was still one too many on the rock and for the time being there was little doubt that it was me. Aenne and Graciela screamed when the massive body began to move about wildly and well over a ton of muscle and flesh whipped through the air. I retreated to the highest point of the rock watching the monster lashing out. I lifted my gun, aimed carefully so that in no circumstances would I miss its head, and pulled the trigger. It needed a second shot before the head was torn to pieces and the snake fell into a hole in the rock.

The rock which marks the frontier between Venezuela and Brazil with prow of authors' boat in foreground (see page 142)

Macu dancers

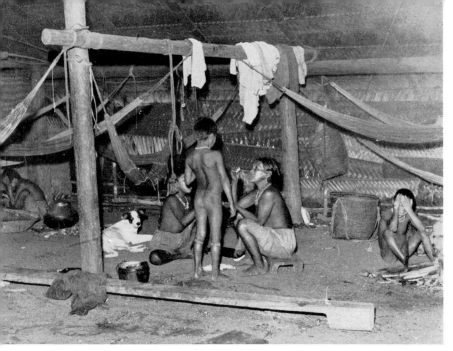

A maloca without partitions

A partitioned maloca

I looked down on the headless giant in its death convulsions and then remembered the boat. Hurriedly I tied it up securely. As quickly as I could I lit a fire and it was not until its warm and comforting glow spread through the darkness that we recovered and became ourselves again. Not far from us the anaconda still twitched and we did not relish the idea of having it with us for the night. We tried to move it but its weight was beyond our strength. Fortunately it moved near to the edge of the rock during its last death throes, so I used a piece of wood to lever the monstrous corpse into the water. It took ages to move but at last, with a cheerful splash, the snake slid from the rock into the water where its huge body sank to the river-bed.

If we thought this was the end we were mistaken. Within a minute or two the water began to boil and swirl as a multitude of fierce and greedy pyranhas with razor-sharp teeth threw themselves on to the carcass. Such was the crazy rapacity of these fish of prey that they tore each other to shreds as well.

We passed a frightful night. Aenne was convinced there must be a second anaconda close by—there had to be for the sake of procreation alone—and she could not relax and go to sleep. The moon rose like a huge red rolling ball about midnight and gave the surrounding scenery a macabre look. Graciela stretched on the bare rock in an exhausted sleep. I asked my wife to roast our last coffee, while I had a little sleep. But she protested energetically and refused to roast the coffee if I slept. At last morning came. The sun rose and our world became normal again. The jungle was covered in sparkling dew drops and shrouded in a transparent mist. As on every other morning, the birds held their concert, the colourful ara birds glided peacefully above us and the howler monkeys opened their screaming chorus. A new day had started and at the bottom of the Casiquiare we could see the sharp clean skeleton of the giant snake about twenty yards long and its size was such that I would have needed both arms to encircle it. We were glad to leave this uncanny place and steer towards new adventure.

I was nervous when I poured the last canister of petrol into the tank of the motor-boat. We had enough to last us to about midday. If we did not reach the Orinoco by then we would be in serious difficulty, since we were sailing up-stream. Once we reached the Orinoco we would be safe, because we could then, if necessary, drift downstream with the river. And so, through the tense morning my brain never stopped hammering in rhythm with the engine, Will it last? . . . or won't it last? . . . in maddening, unceasing repetition. River-bend followed river-bend and there was still no sign of the Orinoco. The Casiquiare became narrower, the current stronger and our progress seemed intolerably slow.

We turned another bend and magically a wide open sea lay before us. It was the light-green waters of the Orinoco slowly rolling downstream. An hour or so later the last drop of petrol exploded with a bang as I was throwing the mooring rope on to the quay of an American missionary post at Tamatameque where a crowd of people had come to welcome the unexpected visitors from nowhere.

12

Chori-Chori

THE hospitable American missionaries at Tamatameque came from the New Tribus sect of Chico, California. They were astounded at our arrival from the interior because they believed their mission station to be at the end of the world, and anything from beyond passed their comprehension.

Unfortunately our smoking disturbed them, as they taught the Indians that a person who believes in God must not smoke, drink or take drugs. The tribes of the Waikas, Guahibos and Maquiritares, who live along the upper reaches of the Orinoco, sniff the pulverised leaves of the coca-bush which they mix with the ashes of the burnt leaves of the guarea tree. They also have a habit of blowing narcotic dust into each other's nostrils through thin hollowed-out bones. They make this dust from certain kinds of liana with which they mix powdered fruit seeds. The result is similar to cocaine snuff.

The head of the mission had been living in this God-forsaken and mosquito-plagued place for ten years without returning to his home in the United States. He was assisted by two families, with a bunch of toddlers and three confirmed bachelors, all from the same sect. The greatest achievement which these missionaries had to show for their devotion was, in my opinion, a series of tape recordings of the different Indian languages.

I asked one of the bachelor missionaries, who had been living in Tamatameque for four years, why he had come to the jungle. He answered that when he embraced The Gospel a few years earlier he became a new person, with the will and strength to face the hardships of Tamatameque, because he knew that God appreciated his sufferings and would reserve a special place in Heaven for him.

These young men had made their home in a completely iso-lated place, as near to hell as any spot on earth could be. They lived and worked in the sticky heat of a permanent Turkish bath, endlessly plagued by mosquitos. Even the Indians avoided this region and lived higher up at the sources of the Orinoco. The missionaries made extensive journeys to this unexplored territory and persuaded whole families with promises and bribes to return with them to Tamatameque. They taught them the Christian faith in a manner that was incomprehensible to the natives.

The Indians love contemplation, long indefinite palavers, music, dancing and drinking; they believe in good and bad demons and aim to win their favour with ancient formulae and rites. They live in constant fear of these demons, and the power of the medicine-man is based almost entirely on this fear. Then a handful of strangers—people who speak a different language, are of different appearance and come from another world—visit their land to try and uproot the natives from their traditional beliefs. They substitute a new 'all-powerful' God, a new belief based on Western values and civilisation, and expect it to work. At first they often succeed in dazzling the Indians with glittering gifts and promises of paradise.

Inborn inquisitiveness will make almost any Indian join this new kind of magic, but very seldom does the missionary succeed in penetrating the thoughts and deeper emotions of the people he hopes to convert. For most of the Indians I have observed these conversions are very much like a play at the theatre; once the curtain has fallen they return to the realities of everyday life. Once the supervising missionary departs, things revert to the way they have been for hundreds and hundreds of years and all that is remembered and discussed are the presents which the missionaries leave behind. At the earliest opportunity the Indians will seek to regain the favours of their old demons by celebrating feasts in their honour. After all, what did the missionary offer apart from the presents? Work for very little pay and total

Caruru Falls, upper Rio Tiquié

Back in civilisation, Caracas

abstention. I think the Indians are still too close to nature to accept such a bargain.

Three days from Tamatameque, up the Orinoco, the territory of the Waikas begins. These people belong to the same group of tribes as the Cauaburys and can be as dangerous to white people. For this reason this whole territory is largely unexplored. This, as usual, was a challenge to us, so we decided to visit them.

We got some petrol from the missionaries and the first evening after our departure we reached the place of Esmeralda—meaning Emerald. This is supposed to be the pearl of the Orinoco and it is marked with a thick blob on every map. We expected to find a large settlement, but to our surprise we found the spot unpopulated; the hellish swarms of mosquitos must have driven everyone away, despite the beauty of the place.

As we climbed a hill in the burning heat, the sweat poured from us, but it was worth it. From the top a panorama of tropical jungle, rivers and snow-clad mountains, as beautiful as anything we had seen on our travels, stretched out before us. Towards the north we could see the eight-thousand-feet-high mountain of Duida—the unbelievable mountain—and behind it the Venezuelan mountain range. Looking west, our eyes followed the Orinoco winding its way through the jungles. In the far distance, we saw the place where the Brazo de la Casiquiare connects the Orinoco with the Rio Negro. To the south was the land of Cauaburys, a vast sea of unexplored, undulating jungle stretching towards Brazil. To the north-west was the wide savannah, broken only by small copses dotted about on the endless plain. Here live the Guahibos Indians, perhaps the most feared natives in Venezuela, who belong to the same group of tribes as the Waika, Cauabury and Macu.

The further upstream we travelled, the faster the Orinoco ran. Eventually it took on the character of a mountain stream and we had to cope with whirlpools, rocks and small rapids. When the river had become narrow we met a large canoe, driven by an outboard motor, coming from the other direction. Five half-naked Indians sat under the palm-leaf roof and at the helm was a man dressed in spotless white trousers, dazzling white shirt and

L

a tropical helmet. I circled the boat, calling 'Chori, Chori'. In the Waika language this means 'brother-in-law' or 'good friend'. It is a term of greeting amongst friends, but it is also used by strangers to signify friendly intentions. The tribe of the Waikas is often referred to as *The Choris*. The Indians stopped their motor and when I called 'Chori, Chori' again they broke into screams of laughter. 'We aren't filthy animals called "*Choris*", we are human beings,' said the man with the tropical helmet. He told us proudly, in good Spanish, that they were Maquiritaris and civilised people and the masters of the region. '*Choris*' were little better than animals that crawled about in the woods, naked. The nearest village of the '*Choris*' lay half a day's journey upstream where the Rio Padamo runs into the Orinoco, he told me. He added that he and his crew lived below Tamatameque and that they were cutting wood for the white people. That explained the outboard motor, the white shirt and tropical helmet. We presented the leader with a pair of fancy earrings and received in return a juicy leg of smoked boar. It was a cheerful meeting on both sides. We now knew where we would find the first Waikas, and sun-helmet and his friends had an interesting topic for later palavers.

It was dark when we tied up for the night. The territory of the Waikas stretched inland on the opposite side of the river and we felt sure that the natives must have heard the noise of our engine. We did not sleep very soundly.

Soon after we had started next morning the first Waika huts came into view at the mouth of a small tributary of the Orinoco. Beside their huts, the naked inhabitants watched us closely. When we were close enough we called 'Chori, Chori' to them and steered a large semicircle in front of the settlement. We heard them call 'Chori, Chori' in answer, then before I had a chance to tie up the boat, they scrambled aboard. Their curiosity seemed boundless.

The only way we could get them to leave the boat was to push them into the water. I pushed the men, Aenne the women and Graciela the children. There was a tense moment when it looked as if the natives would resist, which could have had ugly consequences, but when they saw that we meant business they slowly left the boat of their own accord. I climbed the steep bank to their settlement with them and they seemed happy again. The women and children kept calling and making signs to Graciela and Aenne to come up as well. As soon as Aenne reached the top of the bank the women rushed to get their children and were blissfully happy when my wife took the dirty little bundles in her arms. Unfortunately, language difficulties restricted our conversation.

The men showed me their six-foot bows and arrows which they had fetched from the jungle where they kept them hidden. Now they wanted to exchange them with anything I had, especially clothing. This was understandable since the swarms of mosquitos were a terrible pest even to them. I was tempted by the beautifully worked bows and the six feet tall hardwood arrows, with their exchangeable points. But I did not intend to return to my boat completely naked. Somehow the chief had grabbed my shirt and before I had time to protest he had wound it lovingly round the naked shoulders of a girl, probably his latest wife. My trousers, too, had somehow or other found their way to a new owner.

When the natives realised that I was as naked as they were, they lost what little respect they had had for me and swarmed over the boat again. I rushed back, just in time to save our belongings from disappearing.

The bargaining started. It seemed that the Waikas had a special use for everything; spoons were employed as an adornment for the hair, a towel was used as a little frock for a child, pots became hats, and a strainer a one-side brassiere. Graciela bent double with laughter, but I was not entirely amused as more and more of our goods and chattels disappeared. Soon I was surrounded by bows and arrows which had been given to me in exchange for our things. There were arrows with poisoned points, others with broad points used only for the killing of human beings, others with hooks and poisoned rings for different types of animals. It was high time to cast off, so I tried to explain that we wanted to visit another settlement of the tribe. When they finally understood, the Indians rushed forward to accompany us and show us the way. I managed to drive all the visitors off the boat with the exception of two women who were sitting stark naked on our dining-table nursing babies. It took another hour before I could persuade them, half in sign language and half by physical force, that there simply was no room on our boat for passengers. There really was not an inch to spare. Bows and arrows, baskets, native pots and masks, shields and idols, took up every inch of available space.

When we were once more chugging up the Orinoco we discovered that a great number of things had disappeared. No fishing tackle had been left on board and we had to use our native trophies as cooking utensils.

During the early afternoon we reached a small banana plantation on the left side of the river. At first we thought we would pass it, then decided to turn back. When we did I saw through my binoculars a naked Indian, his bow and arrow at the ready. As our boat came nearer he ran away.

We called 'Chori, Chori' after him and, as if struck by lightning, he stopped. We called again but there was no reply. We tried repeatedly until, slowly, one after another, naked Indians appeared from the jungle. Soon scores of women and children joined them.

The Waikas must have heard our motor for a long time, so we could not have surprised them; but I think they were startled to hear me call their special term of friendly greeting. I could not see any communal huts or individual shelters which might have served as homes, and I came to the conclusion that their settlement was some distance away. These Waikas were reserved, but when they realised we had come as friends, they too stormed our boat like a horde of inquisitive children. They were much more numerous than the previous tribe and I shuddered to think how many more might still be in the jungle. I moved the boat out into the river so that the only way they could get aboard was along a tree trunk. A handful of natives who had made themselves at home on our boat and were rummaging amongst our belongings were expedited back to land that way with a mixture of force and persuasion. Then Graciela and I went ashore while Aenne stayed on the boat to look after our

belongings. As soon as we reached land Graciela became the
centre of attraction, especially with the women and children.
She stood amongst them proud and erect, smiling at her admirers
and condescending to let them touch her blonde hair.

When I saw that Graciela was happy and obviously capable of
looking after herself I looked round for interesting things to
photograph. An attractive girl of about eighteen caught my eye;
she had pretty features and, strangely enough, her weird get-up
did not spoil her good looks. A long bamboo stick pierced both
her nostrils, the lobes of her ears had an inch hole in them to
which large bunches of feathers were fixed, her face, and naked,
well-proportioned body were painted with designs in bright
colours. Her hair had a simply page-boy cut with a tonsure
painted in bright red. She was 'made-up' and 'dressed-up' in
much the same fashion as the other women, but somehow she
seemed different.

While I was photographing this girl, an old man kept pestering
me, obviously wanting me to do or understand something. At
first I thought he had been sent by the medicine-man to prevent
me from taking photographs, but eventually I understood that
he wanted me to move the boat upstream where there is a good
little harbour. Since I had not seen any signs of a settlement so
far, I agreed willingly.

Immediately I returned to the boat, Aenne asked me if I had
seen Graciela. I went back to the banana plantation, but all the
villagers and Graciela had disappeared. The old man, who was
waiting in the boat to show me the way to the harbour, was impatiently gesticulating for me to get going. I called Graciela,
but she did not answer. I felt fairly certain that the women
had enticed her to their settlement and that she would be completely safe, yet once we were on the move I had an awful
sinking feeling, remembering the reputation the Waikas had for
kidnapping women and children.

I tried to persuade myself that such fears were the result of
the strangeness of our surroundings and that the moist damp
heat was telling on me. All the same, as soon as we found the
harbour and tied up, I ran up the steep embankment hoping to

see the settlement. But when I arrived at the top there was not a single hut to be seen, nor a sign of any natives. I turned to call the old man and discovered that he had disappeared somewhere into the thick jungle. Now I was worried.

I fetched my camera with its flashlight attachment from the boat and dashed into the jungle. I soon found a path which led away from the river, and hoping it would lead to a settlement, I followed it. My hunch was right and in a few minutes I reached a clearing where there was a large palm-leaf roof almost growing out of the thick undergrowth.

Smoke was coming from many places and a low muffled murmur rose from below the ground. Not a sound could be heard from the jungle. It was the most eerie place I had come across since we had set out on our travels. Normally, drums, chanting, or a babble of voices could be heard from a native settlement, but this one seemed altogether different. The people seemed to be like animals, or a race from another planet. I had always thought of the natives as people like us but with a different approach to life and different ways of dressing. I had never really felt frightened of them as long as we were able to make them understand that we came as friends and did not intend to change their way of life. But now, not knowing where Graciela was and not having any contact with the people who must have taken her with them, I felt helpless and small in the endless tropical forest.

I crept silently around the big roof until I found an opening. I crawled into it as quietly as I could and reached a large, low room. When my eyes got used to the darkness I found that it was empty except for a cold fireplace and posts with hammocks tied between them. Then I saw a small opening in the matted walls through which one could get into other rooms. The whole place seemed like a rabbit warren or a large underground communal hut.

I heard the crackling of a fire behind one of the partitions and soon discovered an opening. I squeezed through. The first thing I saw in the glow of the little fire was Graciela looking at me with surprise. She was squatting near the fireplace next to a naked Waika who was yawning and stretching himself on a hammock. In another hammock the beautiful girl with the bamboo through her nose sat swinging her arms round a little boy who was probably her son.

In retrospect there was nothing in this family idyll which ought to have caused me to fear for the safety of my daughter. It was most likely that she simply followed the Waikas and was now waiting to be fetched by me. But at that moment I could not take such a detached view, I was convinced that my child was in danger and that immediate action was necessary. Without hesitation I clicked the camera shutter, setting off a flash-bulb into the eyes of the unsuspecting Waika. He jumped from his hammock, shielding his eyes with his forearm. Graciela, who was used to the flashlight, shrieked with delight and flung herself around my neck.

Then a Waika with a quiver of poisoned arrows tied to his back squeezed himself through the opening from an adjacent room. I heard rustling and talking from all around me, and felt that the whole communal hut with its labyrinth of rooms and passages had come to life. I felt trapped and surrounded but I remember thinking how impossible it would be for the Waikas to use their six-feet bows and arrows inside the maze of small rooms. For all that I had only one urge, to escape with my child. Other natives were now trying to get into the room to see what the commotion was about, so I released another flash-bulb and, dragging Graciela behind me, started on a hasty retreat. We squeezed and pushed through hole after hole in the walls of little rooms, some of them empty, others crowded with startled Waika families, until at last we found our way from the dim interior of the hut into the open.

The sun was blinding and the moist hot air wrapped itself around us so that it was difficult to breathe. Yet to me it was like coming up to the surface from a deep dive. Holding hands, Graciela and I ran and stumbled as fast as we could towards the harbour and the safety of our boat. We tore past a group of Indians who stared as if they had seen a ghost, and then called after us. Overwrought by fear, I thought they were ordering us to stop. Then we met a group of chattering Waika women who scattered in all directions when they saw us. No doubt the terror that beset me was mirrored in my face. Graciela caught my agitation; if her father was frightened, something must be wrong. She began whimpering and whining and pleading with me to stop running and tell her what was the matter. But I would not stop until we reached the boat, completely exhausted. Aenne had been watching our desperate flight and was shaking all over. 'Thank God you're back, thank God you're back,' she kept repeating.

The three of us were in such a state of terror that we expected Waika armies to storm down the embankment to prevent us from leaving. We were possessed by one idea—to get away as quickly as possible from these dangerous river banks.

Quite suddenly the old man reappeared, and before I had time to recover from my fright he was sitting astride the bow of the boat holding the tree trunk. He was talking and shouting at me, but although I could not understand a word I imagined that he was threatening us with horrible retribution if we dared to leave.

The old Waika was as strong as a bear and I found it impossible to push him off the boat. Should I hit him over the head with my heavy bush knife? Even in my state of hysteria I felt unable to do so. Then I had a bright idea. I tore my last shirt from my body and held it towards the old Waika, whose eyes began to shine as he stretched out his arms towards me. I took advantage of this moment to push the boat further into the stream, but before we had reached the end of the tree trunk the old man grabbed it again. He had put on my shirt with remarkable speed and was now shouting with strange guttural sounds towards the jungle.

We simply had to get away from this place, whatever the sacrifice. I took off my trousers and handed them to the old man. Again his eyes lit up, and as he reached out with both hands I had an opportunity to push the boat further away from the land. At last we had reached the end of the tree trunk, but the Waika managed to grab it just in time and hold on tightly as the fast flowing stream caught the boat and turned it slowly. I rushed back to the engine and started the motor, but as I was running forward again to set the controls I saw a horde of armed and decorated Waikas storming down the embankment. At first I thought it was my imagination playing tricks on me, but I soon realised that it *was* a Waika horde. A few seconds later and they were balancing on the tree trunk.

I put the controls at full speed and turned the rudder the other way. The power of the engine combined with the speed of the river was too much even for the tough old man, and he fell into the water. In the few moments that the Waika warriors stared in amazement at their comrade struggling in the water, our boat reached the middle of the river. Soon we were speeding towards a bend where the Waikas disappeared from our sight.

Exhausted and trembling we stared at each other. Graciela began to cry and clung to her mother with all the strength of her thin little arms. By promising her that we would now travel straight home away from wild people and the dark jungle, we managed to calm her. And as Aenne and I talked and talked to our daughter, trying to comfort her, we realised that the last few years had completely exhausted us. Like Graciela, all we wanted now was to get home to civilisation, safety and a little security. In spite of the fact that we loved these primitive people, their actions and ways of thinking were so different from ours that we could never feel quite relaxed and secure with them. This constant tension had been slowly undermining our morale and had eventually resulted in something close to a nervous breakdown.

One can never tell, but looking back, I wonder if the Waikas really intended to kidnap our child. There was no doubt that they had invited her to the communal hut. Like all Indian natives, they were very curious and wanted to inspect her at their leisure. It is possible that they did not want her to leave the hut in case she lost herself in the jungle. The old man probably only wanted to be helpful or barter a few pieces of clothing and the hordes of wild Indians running down the embankment may only have wanted to inspect the motor-boat before we left.

But our raw nerves interpreted everything the natives did into actions directed against us. It was time we got back to our civilisation, however imperfect.

13

Journey's End

THE last lap to the Caribbean was not the smooth sailing we had hoped it would be. It was the toughest part of our four years' journey and was like returning tired and exhausted from a cross-country run only to find that an assault course still lay ahead. Looking back at it now, the last few months of our journey have blurred into one long fight with rapids and other obstacles which seemed intent on destroying us before we reached our goal. There were some incidents which remain vivid in my mind.

There was the Santa Barbara waterfall—twenty miles of continuous rapids, dozens of islands and thousands of submerged rocks. We had missed the right waterway and suddenly came upon a waterfall which thundered frighteningly down for twenty or thirty feet. We managed to turn about and avoid disaster, but at the waterfalls of La Muerte—the death—we had perhaps the closest escape of our journey. Feeling our way through a labyrinth of islands and rocks, we found ourselves over a waterfall which sucked us forward inch by inch until the boat overbalanced and was swept into the depths. Diving down, bow first, the boat submerged under the boiling water, until, like a submarine, it forced itself to the surface. Filled with water and the motor out of action, we managed to get aground on a sandbank.

I shall never forget the relief when the driver of a lorry saved us sixty miles of agonising waterfalls when he took us, boat and all, on his truck from Sanariapo to Ayacucho. And I shall always remember one of the nicest characters we met—the boat-builder who offered to repair the hull of our boat which had been damaged when we unloaded it from the truck. It was a Tuesday and the boat-builder said he could not start work until the next Monday. He explained that for the last ten years he had worked only on Mondays; the rest of the week he whiled away fishing, walking, and drinking in moderation. He was very sorry, but he could not change a way of life which had suited him for so long. I was immensely impressed by the philosophy of this Venezuelan—at last we had found a man who knew how to live —even though I did not intend to wait for a week. I set about repairing the damage myself. The boat-builder kept me company, sitting on a tree trunk with a big cigar in his mouth, giving me good advice while I worked.

Dreading the prospect of navigating the formidable San Borchardt waterfalls, we climbed a rock to view the rapid we would soon have to face. From the top we could follow the twisting course of the Orinoco until it disappeared into the horizon. To the south-east the undulating plains of the savannah merged with the mountains in the far distance. To the west, quite close to us, black rugged mountains of huge rocks and boulders were piled on top of each other, cut by deep cracks and canyons, from which green vegetation and giant cacti struggled for light. Opposite, to the east and on the Colombian side of the river, we could see the giant rock, La Ventana—the window—on whose summit there stands a tourist hut built by an Australian, an American and a Czech. It is a place for a perfect holiday. There are guns for hunting, fishing tackle for fishing, a speed-boat for pleasure trips. All one needs is one's wallet. The vast savannah, dotted with woods and copses, is perfect for the hunting of stag, roe, tapir, monkeys, pumas and jaguars. There is a fantastic variety of birds, and almost every kind of fresh-water fish can be caught in the Orinoco. For the lover of nature this is paradise and it is only a few hours by air and boat from Bogota to La Ventana.

It was understandable that the never-ending succession of rapids depressed Aenne. As soon as she was in the boat she became taut and nervous. When we came in sight of a rapid she would scream and bury her head in her hands. She had never lost her fear of the river and the rapids terrified her even more than the tropical thunderstorms. Sometimes I had to leave the wheel to adjust the engine and Aenne had to take over. It was never long before her hands began to shake and she headed us straight for the nearest rock. Often I was only just in time to tear her cramped fingers from the steering wheel and get the boat on the right course again. She calmed down only when we went ashore.

We were making good progress down the river when out of the blue a shot whizzed past our boat. A few moments later a speedboat pulled alongside and a man in uniform told us excitedly that we were under arrest. We were escorted to the river bank where a group of exotically dressed people—some of them in uniform—awaited us. They were screaming and gesticulating wildly. One man who wore an embroidered open-neck shirt which scarcely hid the abundant black hair on his chest, performed a war-dance round us. We had to wait for them to calm down before we could discover our crime. It appeared that we had taken a forbidden channel between two sandbanks which was a reserved turtle breeding ground let to a trading company. Two barges, with crews, had been standing by for two weeks awaiting the moment when thousands of turtles would invade the sandbanks to lay their eggs. We were accused of having driven them away with our motor-boat. I apologised profusely and then demanded the food which, I claimed, was the right of any prisoner. We were given a good meal and when I had convinced the authorities that we had no money to pay for it, they lost all interest in us and let us go. From then on when we saw sandbanks marked with a bamboo stick from which fluttered a white handkerchief, we carefully avoided them.

Soon after that incident we ran into strong head winds that blew and whistled past us. At river bends and steep embankments where the current ran faster, the winds caused high waves and breakers. The natives called them *burros montados*—mounted donkeys—and they plagued us terribly. At times the waves were six-feet high and one of them caught at a wrong angle could fill our heavily laden boat with water. In the end we were restricted to travelling one hour in the morning and two hours in the afternoon, when for some strange reason the wind dropped.

Somehow we could no longer enjoy the scenery and the simplicity of our life. The traffic on the river was increasing daily, quite often there were aeroplanes overhead, and the people we met had close contact with the outside world. All we wanted to do now was to get our journey finished as quickly as possible. But our progress was very slow. One day I became impatient and stayed on the river too long. The two hours of calm water had passed and the *burros montados* tossed us about and the waves broke right over the boat. Aenne was sitting next to me staring silently into the river and baling mechanically, when an especially large wave broke over us. She began sobbing hysterically and saying that she could stand it no longer.

I could not leave the steering wheel as the waves needed constant evasive action, but Graciela put her arms around her mother and comforted her. 'We will soon be back, Mummy,' she said. 'We will live in our own little house in the country and we will never have to travel again.' But Aenne could not stop and soon Graciela was crying as desperately as her mother. I steered towards land and carried Aenne up the steep bank into the forest where she could neither see nor hear the river.

From then on we camped only on those sandbanks that faced land, thus giving our nerves a chance to recuperate from the cruel persistence of the river. We spent the nights stretched out on the hot sand, covered with our hammocks, and awoke in the morning with our noses, mouths and ears filled with sand. Slowly Aenne recovered, but she still hated the water and the waves drove her to desperation. But she made up her mind never to break down again and heroically endured the rest of the journey.

On the day we tied up for the night at Los Dragos we saw a distant spread of light reflected in the sky that made our hearts beat faster with anticipation. Bolivar! This was the first sign of a new life and the end of our journey. We lay down on a sandbank that night with the reflections of thousands of electric lights reminding us that we were spending our last night in the open.

All three of us were jubilant that the trip was over. The last part of the journey had been the most terrible strain. The suffering of Aenne, and Graciela's unhappiness at seeing her mother so upset, together with the responsibility for their safety, had worn me down and for a long time I had wished the journey to end. Aenne had lived in a nightmarish world during the last few weeks and only her will-power and the knowledge that there would be an end to her sufferings had kept her going. That moment had now come and she lay on her back on the sand looking at the glow in the sky, radiant with relief and happiness.

For Graciela, too, this was an important moment. She had grown up a lot in the past weeks and had begun to understand that our unsettled life and never-ending wanderings were not all fun and games. She had also learned by watching her mother what suffering and anguish meant and the idea of danger had become very real to her.

It would be difficult to describe the intense emotions we experienced that night. We were about to start a new and different life again and in some ways it felt as it did five years ago when we stood at the railing of the ship watching the lights of Caracas.

The harbour authorities of Bolivar required every boat driven by an engine to have a name. So we named our boat *Casiquiare* and hoisted the Peruvian flag at the stern. It was the first time that a boat which had its home at the source of the Amazon in southern Peru had reached Bolivar by water. It was so unusual that no one noticed it and no newspaper thought it worthwhile to print a single line about us. As far as the Venezuelans were concerned the Orinoco finished at the Ayacucho Falls.

We decided to end our journey at Bolivar, the largest town on the Orinoco before it reaches the Caribbean sea through an enormous delta of waterways used by the largest steamers. It would have been senseless to make this journey in our uncomfortable little craft simply for the sake of reaching the sea.

So the three of us sat on a bench opposite a soup kitchen and divided our last banana, without a centimo in our pockets. Our eyes followed with longing the plates of hot food which were handed out for only one bolivar to anyone who was hungry. Graciela and Aenne said nothing but I knew what they felt. I pulled myself together and went to see the president of the municipal government in his impressive office. This important dignitary listened to my proposition and agreed to let me have the municipal theatre to exhibit my photographs, the thousand-year-old materials and household utensils of the Incas, and the arms and other things we had brought back from the interior.

The entrance fee was small, but few people came; the citizens of Bolivar were more interested in oil, iron, gold and diamonds than in their exalted forefathers or their primitive brethren. On my departure the municipal president handed me a few banknotes so that we were not entirely destitute. The owner of the largest metal business in Bolivar, a fellow-countryman of mine, transported us with our boat and belongings, free of charge, on one of his giant lorries, four hundred miles to Caracas, the starting point of our journey.

In Caracas, our four-year trip across the entire continent ended on the terrace of the famous American department store, Sears Roebuck. Here the *Casiquiare* was exhibited and our trophies and photographs displayed in an adjacent room. The French showed the greatest interest, but our own countrymen stood for a long time in front of the ticket desk wondering whether to spend a bolivar on the exhibition. More often than not they decided that a bottle of Coca-Cola would be a safer investment.

The Venezuelans in Caracas seemed more interested in our exhibition than their countrymen in Bolivar. Newspapers and television reported our journey, and I was asked to lecture. But one noticed the discomfort of many Venezuelans at having their primitive brothers from the interior publicly exhibited. Caracas had become such an industrialised city—a boom town bent on wealth and progress—that its inhabitants were not interested in the greatness of their distant past and were embarrassed by my stories of primitive life.

In spite of the fact that we had earned very little money and that our future was as insecure as ever, Aenne was happy and quickly learned to laugh again. There was something new every day. We were invited to private houses, cinemas, to appear on television; we could walk around the fabulous and exciting city, window-shopping. People began to recognise us and it happened quite often that Aenne was stopped in the streets with the greeting: '*Ola, Indiana blanca, come esta?*'—'Hallo, white Indian, how are you?' Graciela enjoyed showing people round the exhibition; a duty which she performed with a self-assurance that was amazing for a child of ten. She had become rather serious through the long journey, more reflective and sensitive than other children of her age, and yet, in some ways, more childish. If anybody asked her whether she wanted to go back to the Indians she was quite definite in saying that she would not like it, not even if her father and mother went again. And yet she would tell friends how nice the trip had been. I think Aenne's attitude was similar; at first she could not bear the thought of another expedition to the interior, but when she began to forget the hardships and drudgery the spell of the tropical jungle remained and the idea of going back appealed to her again.

After the exhibition we travelled to Europe where I hoped to find people more interested in my venture. But all I found were slaves of time running around in circles. Out of bed at seven in the morning, gulping down their breakfast, rushing for the bus to become part of the vast machinery of mass production; a short lunch break, a longing glance at the warm sun and back to work, to routine and mediocrity. I, too, was caught by the rush and the hurry. I fought in the ante-rooms to see important people who had no time to spare and who did not understand me. I hurried to Genoa, Milan, Basle, Munich, Stuttgart, Frankfurt, Hamburg and London to lecture about the things I had learned and experienced, but my words fell on dead, tired ears.

We soon realised that life in Europe did not suit us and we decided to return to South America. In spite of our hardships, it seemed as if the vast continent with its many races, its strange magic and conflicting cultures, its endless unspoilt nature, had cast a lasting spell on me. Our four years' journey had taught me that I could not run away from civilisation for ever, but the last few months had also convinced me that I belonged to the country of the Amazon and the Orinoco. Maybe I am doomed to remain the eternal vagabond.